A-LEVEL STUDENT GUIDE

OCR

Sociology

Researching and understanding social inequalities

Katherine Roberts
Steve Chapman

HODDER EDUCATION
AN HACHETTE UK COMPANY

This Guide has been written specifically to support students preparing for the OCR A-level Sociology examinations. The content has been neither approved nor endorsed by OCR and remains the sole responsibility of the authors.

Every effort has been made to trace all copyright holders, but if any have been inadvertently overlooked, the Publishers will be pleased to make the necessary arrangements at the first opportunity.

Although every effort has been made to ensure that website addresses are correct at time of going to press, Hodder Education cannot be held responsible for the content of any website mentioned in this book. It is sometimes possible to find a relocated web page by typing in the address of the home page for a website in the URL window of your browser.

Hachette UK's policy is to use papers that are natural, renewable and recyclable products and made from wood grown in well-managed forests and other controlled sources. The logging and manufacturing processes are expected to conform to the environmental regulations of the country of origin.

Orders: please contact Bookpoint Ltd, 130 Park Drive, Milton Park, Abingdon, Oxon OX14 4SE. Telephone: (44) 01235 827827. Fax: (44) 01235 400401. Email: education@bookpoint.co.uk. Lines are open from 9 a.m. to 5 p.m., Monday to Saturday, with a 24-hour message answering service. You can also order through our website: www.hoddereducation.co.uk.

© Katherine Roberts and Steve Chapman 2020

ISBN 978-1-5104-7206-8

First printed 2020

First published in 2020 by
Hodder Education,
An Hachette UK Company
Carmelite House
50 Victoria Embankment
London EC4Y 0DZ

www.hoddereducation.co.uk

Impression number   10 9 8 7 6 5 4 3 2 1

Year   2024 2023 2022 2021 2020

All rights reserved. Apart from any use permitted under UK copyright law, no part of this publication may be reproduced or transmitted in any form or by any means, electronic or mechanical, including photocopying and recording, or held within any information storage and retrieval system, without permission in writing from the publisher or under licence from the Copyright Licensing Agency Limited. Further details of such licences (for reprographic reproduction) may be obtained from the Copyright Licensing Agency Limited, www.cla.co.uk

Cover photo: verve/Adobe Stock.

Typeset by Integra Software Services Pvt. Ltd, Pondicherry, India

Printed in Dubai

A catalogue record for this title is available from the British Library.

Contents

Getting the most from this book 4
About this book 5

Content Guidance

Section A Research methods and researching social inequalities

What is the relationship between theory and methods? 6
What are the main stages of the research process? 10
Which methods are used in sociological research? 19

Section B Understanding social inequalities

Social inequality and social class 31
Social inequality and gender 40
Social inequality and ethnicity 49
Social inequality and age 59

Questions & Answers

How to use this section 69
The A-level examination 71
Example 1 questions 72
Example 2 questions 80
Example 3 questions 90

Knowledge check answers 99
Index 101

Getting the most from this book

Exam tips

Advice on key points in the text to help you learn and recall content, avoid pitfalls, and polish your exam technique in order to boost your grade.

Knowledge check

Rapid-fire questions throughout the Content Guidance section to check your understanding.

Knowledge check answers

1 Turn to the back of the book for the Knowledge check answers.

Summaries

- Each core topic is rounded off by a bullet-list summary for quick-check reference of what you need to know.

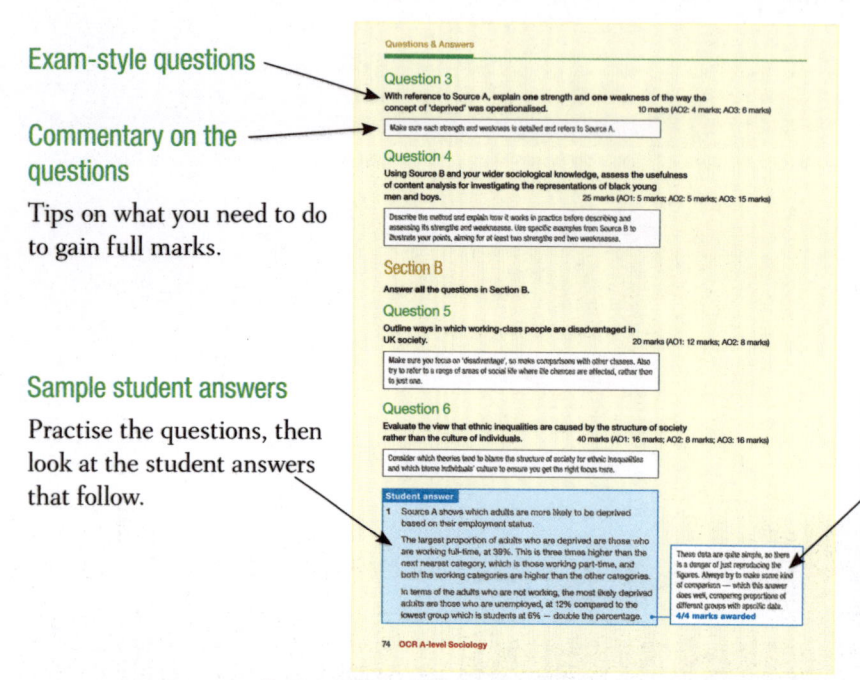

Exam-style questions

Commentary on the questions

Tips on what you need to do to gain full marks.

Sample student answers

Practise the questions, then look at the student answers that follow.

Commentary on sample student answers

Read the comments showing how many marks each answer would be awarded in the exam and exactly where marks are gained or lost.

About this book

This guide covers Component 2: Researching and understanding social inequalities in the OCR Sociology specification H580 (A-level).

How to use this book

The first main section of the book is **Content Guidance**. It follows the headings for Researching and understanding social inequalities in the OCR specification. Each part of the Content Guidance contains exam tips, knowledge checks and definitions of some key terms. Knowing and understanding the meaning of sociological concepts is an essential part of the whole course.

The second main section of the book is **Questions & Answers**. At the beginning of this section are the three assessment objectives (AOs) against which your exam answers will be judged, with some guidance regarding how to display the required skills, and a list of command words, which will help you to understand more clearly what each question is asking you to do. The questions provided are in the style of the OCR exam for Component 2, and are each followed by an A-grade answer. Remember the importance of noting the structure and mark allocations of questions. Throughout the student answers, you will find comments explaining why what has been written is good and is scoring well. More detailed guidance on how to use the Questions & Answers section is given on pages 69–71.

Content Guidance

■ Section A Research methods and researching social inequalities

What is the relationship between theory and methods?

Positivism

Positivists argue that social behaviour is the product of social forces beyond the control of the individual. The origin of these social forces or laws lies in the way societies are organised, that is, their social structure. Positivists argue that the social structure of society shapes or determines the behaviour of human beings. In this way, people are the puppets of society.

Positivists highlight the predictability of human actions by identifying social patterns and trends in behaviour. For example, they note that the mass of working-class people generally behave in similar ways with regard to family life, educational achievement, consumption of consumer goods, leisure and cultural pursuits and so on, to the extent that there are clear working-class patterns of behaviour that contrast greatly with middle- or upper-class behaviour.

In light of this, positivists believe that society and the social forces that underpin it should be studied using scientific research methods, on a large scale. There are a number of principles that underpin this scientific approach.

Quantitative data

Positivists value the collection and use of quantitative, or numerical, data that can be converted into graphs, tables and charts, which allow them to identify correlations between patterns and trends. Positivists prefer to use large-scale survey methods that employ questionnaires and/or structured interviews as their primary research method because these are supposedly scientific in character. Additionally, they would value the use of official statistics because these are normally the result of standardised, reliable and objective data collection.

Patterns and trends

When quantitative data have been gathered, they will be analysed for any patterns and/or trends they might show by positivist researchers.

Patterns in the data are links between variables — for example, patterns in relation to ethnic groups, gender or age groups. The researcher may look to see whether the data show that males have different outcomes to females, or whether members of certain

> **Knowledge check 1**
> What is the difference between patterns and trends?

ethnic groups are more likely to do certain things than those of other ethnic groups. It may be that the data just show random connections and no patterns can be identified.

Trends relate to changes over time, so if data are longitudinal in nature (see below for an explanation of longitudinal studies) or if statistics are gathered annually and can be compared, then trends might be identified. There may be an increase or decrease in poverty, unemployment levels or certain crimes, for example.

Objectivity and value freedom

It is important for positivists that the research is carried out **objectively** to ensure that bias does not undermine the research findings. Value freedom is the idea that all sources of bias have been eliminated from the research process. For example, the research design needs to ensure that if the researcher is using a questionnaire or interview, the questions are neutral — they should not reflect any personal, political or sociological position that might lead research subjects into giving certain responses. The researcher also needs to ensure that their interpretation of data is objective — they should avoid being selective when analysing and evaluating their data. Thus, the values of a researcher will have no impact on the research or its findings.

However, the notion of value freedom is a contentious one because critics argue that sociology is social knowledge that is underpinned by sociological perspectives, moral codes, prejudices and, therefore, bias. For example, most sociology reflects Western, capitalist and **patriarchal values**. Interpretivists (see below) would argue that sociology is composed of values because sociologists are members of society and thus cannot escape the influence of its culture and its institutions. They would argue that this should be accepted and recognised.

Reliability

The key research concept of reliability relates to the way the research or measurement process is designed. If the research design is reliable, it generally means that if it is used by other researchers on a similar group of people, the same or similar results should be produced. This would be possible if the design included standardised procedures, which could easily be replicated. Therefore research methods such as structured interviews or questionnaires, which have a set list of questions in a particular order, would be seen as reliable. Reliability is particularly important to positivists, who want to carry out scientific research and who wish to generate data that can be quantified and compared in order to uncover patterns and trends.

However, reliability may be undermined by the fact that some types of research method, notably unstructured interviews and participant observation, often depend on the quality of the personal relationship established between the researcher and the research subjects. It may be impossible for other sociologists to replicate these unique relationships. Additionally, such methods will lack a structured set of questions or standardised procedures, making replication impossible.

Interpretivism

Interpretivists do not believe that human behaviour is predictable or that it is shaped by social laws or social forces over which people have no control. They argue that people have free will and can therefore exercise choice and make decisions to pursue their own courses of action. Individuals are therefore active rather than passive.

> **Exam tip**
>
> The notion that value freedom is virtually impossible to achieve is important when discussing the relationship between sociology and social policy. Do link this to the theoretical debate between positivists and interpretivists and what they are trying to achieve when conducting research.

Objective Refers to lack of bias or influence. Studying something objectively means recording results without influencing the research process or making personal judgements.

Patriarchal values These are ideas that support and maintain male dominance.

> **Exam tip**
>
> Reliability is a key concept to use when evaluating research methods, as is validity (see below). Make sure you have a clear understanding of its meaning and link to positivism and quantitative data.

> **Knowledge check 2**
>
> Explain why reliability is important to a positivist.

Content Guidance

They create their own destinies rather than having them shaped by social structures. Interpretivists' aim in conducting research is to understand the meanings of experiences to individuals, rather than to generalise more widely or make predictions.

Qualitative data

Interpretivists prefer qualitative to quantitative data. Qualitative data are made up of personal accounts taken directly from the subjects of sociological research in the form of interview transcriptions, descriptions of events experienced through participant observations, and so on. This type of data tends to focus on how the research subjects see or interpret the world around them and consequently it often provides insight into the feelings, opinions, motivations and thoughts of those being researched.

Meanings and experiences

Interpretivists consider the social world to be socially constructed — it is the product of shared interaction and the meanings or interpretations that humans use to make sense of that interaction. The role of sociologists is to uncover these shared interpretations or 'meanings', to document social experience and identify the motives and reasons for social actions.

Verstehen, empathy and rapport

Interpretivists argue that the aim of sociological research should be to get inside people's heads and to experience the world from their point of view. This is called empathetic understanding or **verstehen**. Interpretivists therefore emphasise the use of ethnographic methods such as unstructured interviews and participant observation, which aim to conduct research in the research subject's natural environment. Interpretivists also emphasise the importance of establishing a rapport with the respondent. A rapport means a relationship which is based on trust and respect, and if a rapport is established, the responses in an interview situation are likely to be much more valid.

Verstehen Literally 'to understand'. It refers to the ability of the social researcher to understand the social world and action from the respondent's perspective, and 'see through their eyes', using methods such as unstructured interviews, participant observation.

Validity

The key research concept of validity relates to whether research and its findings give a 'true picture' of what is being studied, that is, whether research reflects the reality of the activities or attitudes of the person/group being studied. Validity is especially important to interpretivists, who want to understand the motives and meanings that people attach to their actions. Research which generates detailed, qualitative data is often seen as being more valid, since it gives a more meaningful insight into how the respondents really feel or act.

However, validity can be undermined by a number of factors, including issues of social desirability — where the respondent gives a more socially acceptable answer rather than telling the truth about how they really feel. The personal characteristics of the researcher, and the rapport they have built with the respondent, may also impact on validity, as may issues of **researcher imposition** in, for example, the way the researcher designs their questions or by the way they react to things said, their facial expressions or in the way they interpret the information gained.

Researcher imposition The tendency of a researcher to impose their ideas, values and expectations on the research process as a whole and on the respondent.

Subjectivity, researcher imposition and reflexivity

Interpretivists argue that researcher imposition is an important source of bias in positivist sociological research. That is, when developing research tools, researchers often make decisions or have assumptions about what is and is not important based on their own experience rather than that of the research subjects. Consequently, they may miss something important. Positivists would tend to argue that by maintaining objectivity and value freedom, researcher imposition will be avoided.

Interpretivists argue that their approach of putting the research subjects at the centre of the research is a better way of avoiding this problem. However, critics point out that there is always the danger, in research involving the establishment of rapport and close relationships with subjects, that the sociologist may 'go native' and allow their subjective relationships to overcome their detachment and objectivity. There is also the danger that **subjectivity** might intrude into the research process in the form of selective interpretation of the data because the researcher sympathises with the lifestyle of the group being studied.

Interpretivists tend to be aware of this possibility of bias and have stressed the importance of reflexivity. This refers to researchers being aware of how their decisions and actions may impact on the social behaviour of their subjects during the research process. In order to improve the validity of their findings, many researchers keep a journal of the research process in which they critically self-reflect on their research design and everyday experience of contact with their subjects. A reflexive researcher will also often ask their respondents what impact they feel taking part in the research has had on them, in order to fully acknowledge the two-way nature of social research.

Representativeness and generalisability

Although mentioned in the specification as part of this section, these concepts, which relate more to sampling, will be discussed later in this Guide, under 'The sampling process'.

> **Knowledge check 3**
>
> How is the problem of researcher imposition linked to value freedom?

> **Subjectivity** The opposite of objectivity. In research terms it refers to a researcher interpreting something from their own viewpoint, and becoming personally involved. Although it is not desirable, interpretivists would argue that subjectivity is inevitable.

> **Exam tip**
>
> Much of the debate about the strengths and weaknesses of research methods reflects the debate about whether to take a positivist or interpretivist approach to the investigation of social life. Work this positivist–interpretivist distinction into your answers whenever you can.

Summary

- There are two important theoretical approaches to sociological research: positivism and interpretivism.
- Positivists believe that social behaviour is largely the product of social forces that originate in the social structure or organisation of society.
- Positivists believe that sociologists should use scientific methods that are standardised, reliable, objective and value free in order to identify patterns and trends in behaviour.
- They use methods such as questionnaire surveys and structured interviews which use representative samples and produce quantitative data.
- In contrast, interpretivists believe that social behaviour is the result of people actively choosing to interact in social groups and the interpretations or social meanings that people apply to those encounters.
- Interpretivists stress the importance of validity, arguing that research methods should produce qualitative data that reflect authentic and natural behaviour as well as achieving *verstehen* and building a rapport.
- Interpretivists therefore prefer methods such as unstructured or semi-structured interviews and participant observation.

Content Guidance

What are the main stages of the research process?

Key concepts in the research process

Factors influencing the choice of research topic

The choice of research topic may be influenced by several issues.

Theoretical approach and personal interest

Many sociologists will agree with a particular theory, such as feminism, Marxism or postmodernism. This will influence the topic on which they will tend to focus. For example, a Marxist is likely to be interested in social class inequalities, and a feminist in gender issues. Interactionists often focus on power relationships, which may involve some form of labelling, such as those between teachers and pupils, or between the police and young people.

The researcher's personal interests, often based on their experiences, may also influence their choice of topic. For example, several of the researchers you may have come across in the topic of disability and identity (Component 1) are themselves disabled, and many of the sociologists who investigate issues of racism and ethnic inequalities (considered later in this Guide) are from a minority ethnic background.

Current social problems or issues

Much sociological research is influenced by the important issues of the time, so when levels of unemployment, poverty or crime are high, these are more likely to be topics that are studied by sociologists. Current areas of particular interest to sociologists include issues relating to aspects of identity, and also the influence of the internet and social media on society and individuals.

Funding

Much sociological research is carried out within university departments, and the department might drive the agenda of any research. Other funding organisations may include charities, the Economic and Social Research Council and even the government. Those providing the funding can determine the topic area to be researched. For example, the Joseph Rowntree Foundation is a social policy research charity that focuses on poverty, therefore any research they commission and fund will be related to this area.

Issues of access

Though a sociologist may wish to research a particular area of interest, this may not prove possible due to the problem of access. For example, if wishing to research the backgrounds of those who commit serious crimes, it may be difficult to gain access to prisons in order to interview such people. Similarly, victims of serious crimes may also be hard to track down and persuade to take part. This may impact on topic choice.

Aims, hypothesis and research questions

The aims of a piece of research are the things the researcher is intending to find out about. There will often be between one and three aims which a researcher is trying to achieve. For example, a researcher may aim to uncover links between gender and youth crime, and also aim to discover whether gender affects the likelihood of joining a gang.

Knowledge check 4

Use another example to illustrate the difference between research aims, a hypothesis and research questions.

A hypothesis is a predictive statement, usually based on prior knowledge, which predicts what is expected to be found. This hypothesis can then be proved or disproved in the course of the research. If researching the above aim, a suitable hypothesis may be:

- 'Young males are more likely to become involved in gangs than young females.'

It is more likely that positivists will start with a hypothesis, since they are approaching research in a more scientific manner, and proving or disproving a stated hypothesis tends to be an approach used in scientific research.

Research questions are usually more detailed than aims, and the researcher may generate five or six research questions relating to the aims. For example:

1. Do young males feel more pressure to join gangs than young females?
2. What effects do the media representations of gangs have on young males?
3. Is social class more of an indicator of youth crime than gender?

Operationalisation

An important part of the research process involves the researcher breaking down the aims and/or hypothesis into something that can be consistently measured. This process is known as **operationalisation**. For example, the hypothesis 'Working-class people are less likely to experience upward social mobility' gives rise to three questions of operationalisation:

- What is meant by 'working-class'? This is the research population to be studied so it is important to be precise as to who should be included in this group.
- Are 'less likely' than who? It is important to precisely identify the social group that will be compared with the research population.
- What is meant by 'upward social mobility'? It is important to identify a range of indicators of upward social mobility.

It is also vital that central concepts used in questions are operationalised to ensure that everyone is responding to them in the same way. Researchers use indicators to break down such concepts, enabling them to ask much more specific and standardised questions rather than asking about the concept itself, which may well be understood differently by each respondent. For example, asking people what social class they are from may give a range of answers based on different criteria, because respondents may each interpret social class in a different way. Responses to such questions are therefore worthless, and good researchers will ensure that they break down potentially vague concepts into clear indicators, to make them fully testable and measurable.

Operationalisation is an important part of the research process. Precise measurement of social phenomena cannot occur without it. Positivists require it as it assists reliability — ensuring that all responses are standardised and allowing other researchers to use the same operationalisation criteria. It also aids objectivity because the operationalisation process should weed out potential bias, for example in the design of the questions, ensuring that all respondents interpret questions in the same way.

Operationalisation
The practical process of turning a concept or research aim into something that can be consistently measured. For example, social class can be measured via various indicators, such as occupation, income, lifestyle and housing.

Knowledge check 5
Why might interpretivists be less concerned about the precise operationalising of concepts they are investigating?

Exam tip
Operationalisation is often asked about in exam questions. Make sure you look at the research in the relevant source, determine which concepts require operationalisation and consider which indicators have been or might be used.

Content Guidance

Primary and secondary data

Primary data are gathered 'first-hand' by the sociologist using a variety of methods, for example, asking people questions via questionnaires or interviews, or observing their behaviour.

Secondary data are data that have been collected or produced by another person or organisation for other purposes. For example, official statistics relating to the life chances of people from specific social classes, ethnic groups and men and women are collected by the government, in the form of statistics on crime, unemployment, poverty and educational achievement. Journalists may research poverty or inequality and publish their findings in the form of a newspaper or magazine article, and other research organisations may conduct their own studies. Sociologists may wish to use this type of data, but must be aware that they have had no control over its collection, and therefore be alert for any bias or weaknesses in the data.

Data collection

The data collection stage refers to the actual carrying out of the research — delivering the questionnaires or conducting the interviews or observations, for example. Research methods are considered later in the section, but the data collection process will also include other considerations.

Pilot studies

Before carrying out the research on a large scale, many researchers will conduct a pilot study in order to iron out any potential problems with the questions and/or the ways interviews are conducted. Pilot studies are a 'trial run' of the main research and are tested on a relatively small number of people who have similar characteristics to those who will constitute the main sample. A pilot study is useful because it can check whether questions are clear, unambiguous and free from bias, and that those taking part are interpreting the questions in the same way. A pilot study can also ensure that the research design has successfully identified the 'right' types of people as the research subjects and that the data produced are the required kind.

Knowledge check 6

For which kinds of methods would a pilot study be more or less important?

Interpretation of data

Once the data have been collected, the findings will then need to be interpreted and analysed. Positivists believe it is important that the interpretation of data should be carried out objectively and that data should not be selected simply because they support the hypothesis. They would seek to identify patterns and trends, and thus are likely to present data in the form of tables or graphs, to make the findings easily identifiable.

Interpretivists are likely to have gathered qualitative data, which may be in the form of detailed transcripts from semi-structured or unstructured interviews, or lengthy descriptions from observations. Such data will be presented and interpreted differently from quantitative data — it is unlikely that patterns and trends will be sought. Instead interpretivists will identify themes and categorise their findings accordingly. They will tend to include quotes from the respondents themselves. The process of selecting from the vast amount of qualitative data is potentially problematic and subject to researcher imposition. The use of respondent validation and reflexivity is a response to this problem.

Respondent validation

Respondent validation is a method used to double-check the validity of the data collected. For example, it is sometimes used to check whether the sociological interpretation of why certain attitudes have been expressed during an interview, and the key points the respondent was trying to make, is supported by the respondents themselves. It is based on the acknowledgement that sociologists often come from different backgrounds to the people they are studying and that their upbringing and education may mean they are ill-equipped to understand the behaviour they are researching. It is also a response to a common critique of sociological research that the sociologist often ends up imposing their interpretation of reality on the behaviour of the group being studied — an aspect of 'researcher imposition'. Respondent validation aims to address these problems that potentially undermine the validity, or truth, of the data collected.

Respondent validation aims to improve the authenticity of the collected data by asking a sample of the research subjects whether the sociological interpretation of their behaviour and motives equates with the reality of why they behaved or answered in the way they did. Research subjects are invited to answer further questions, perhaps as part of a follow-up, unstructured interview, or, if the research is observation-based, the observer may engage a person in an informal conversation in an attempt to understand the motives for that person's behaviour.

Knowledge check 7

What approach to research (positivism or interpretivism) is more likely to adopt respondent validation?

Longitudinal studies

Some sociological research is longitudinal in nature. This involves returning to the same respondents at regular intervals during a long time period. Such surveys are useful because they can provide a clear image of changes in attitudes and behaviour over a number of years. For example, the National Child Development Study has followed the same 40,000 children all born in one week in March 1958. Follow-up surveys have tracked the group at intervals and given sociologists fascinating insights into the influence of class, education and family on life chances. There are other well-known examples of longitudinal studies made by documentary companies — for example, the *World in Action* 'Up' programmes or the BBC's *Child of Our Time*. One benefit of such an approach is that it will produce more valid data, since you are not asking people to remember how they felt or acted in the past, but are finding out about such things at the time when they occur.

However, such studies can be problematic. Respondents may drop out or die or the researchers may lose track of them — referred to as the rate of attrition. This may undermine the representativeness of the original sample. It may be that the views of those that remain in the sample may be significantly different to those of the subjects that drop out. Objectivity is also hard to maintain as researchers get to know their subjects over time.

It is important to note that a longitudinal study is not related to a specific method but rather to how it is carried out. You could do a more qualitative longitudinal study, using unstructured interviews every few years, or you could construct a more quantitative study which collects statistical data or involves questionnaires.

Content Guidance

The relationship between sociology and social policy

Social policy refers to attempts by governments to influence how society is organised and how members of society should behave by bringing in new laws, guidelines and controls. Social policy is often aimed at bringing about social change, and sociological research is often used to demonstrate the need for certain social policies or to evaluate their impact.

There are essentially two perspectives with regard to the relationship between sociology and social policy. The first suggests that the job of sociologists is merely to collect evidence on behalf of social policymakers but it is no concern of the sociologist how those data are used. We have to trust that the social policymaker uses the sociological data for the good of all members of society and, even if they do not, sociologists do not have the moral responsibility to ensure social policymakers use the data properly. From this perspective, sociologists are merely disinterested and objective pursuers of facts and truth.

In contrast, the second perspective suggests sociologists need to take responsibility for how their work is translated into social policy because society is characterised by conflicts of interest between different social groups. Some of these wield tremendous power and may be the cause of the social problems identified by sociologists. Therefore, some sociologists have argued that the point of sociology is not just to interpret the world but to challenge its organisation and change it for the better.

The sampling process

Target population

When conducting research, a sociologist will normally be focusing on a particular section of society. It may be all adults in the UK, but it may be more focused — for example, all women in a particular age group or all males from a particular minority ethnic group. Research is also often focused on certain areas of the country. The overall group that the research is focused on, about whom the researcher will then intend to make claims based on their research findings, is referred to as the **target population**. It is usually too expensive and time-consuming to ask everybody in the target population to take part in research. Most researchers select a sample that is representative (i.e. a typical cross section) of the target population they are interested in. With a representative sample, it is possible to generalise the findings of the research to the target population: what is true of the sample should be true of the target population as a whole.

Representativeness

It is important that the sample of people the research is carried out with is representative of the target population. This means the sample should be made up of people who reflect the characteristics of the larger population in terms of social class, age, gender, ethnicity and so on. If the researcher fails to ensure that the sample group participating in the research is representative, then the findings will not be applicable to the wider target population.

Generalisability

Sociologists use representative samples because they normally want to generalise about the behaviour and attitudes of the target population being studied, of which the

---

Target population This refers to the whole group or category of people in society that the research relates to, and to whom the research findings will be applied.

Exam tip

It is common for students to mix up representativeness and generalisability or use them in the wrong way. Representativeness relates to the sample — it is nothing to do with the research methods you then use with this sample. Generalisability relates to what you can do with the findings of your research if your sample is representative.

sample is a typical cross section. They want to say that because the sample behaves or thinks in a particular way, it is highly likely that people similar to those included in the sample will also behave/think in this way. Thus, research which is carried out on a representative sample is usually claimed to be generalisable — the findings of the research are applicable to the whole target population.

Sampling frame

A sampling frame is a list of names of all or most of the people in a particular target population. Examples could include the electoral register (if your target population is all adults in the UK), the postcode address file (which could be useful for a target population from a certain region), school or college registers (if your target population is the students in a particular school or college), GP patient records and club membership lists. All sampling frames are unsatisfactory in some respect — not everyone is included, they are often out of date and some groups may be over-represented while other groups may not be included.

Knowledge check 8
Suggest a suitable sampling frame if your target population is people in your area who keep fit.

Sampling techniques

Random sampling techniques

There are two main techniques available to sociologists to select their sample: random and non-random. Random sampling techniques require a sampling frame from which to select the names 'at random' — meaning that every name has an equal chance of being selected and there is no **selection bias**.

Selection bias Where the researcher shows bias or discrimination when they are selecting their sample, perhaps choosing people they know, people who look friendly, or people who are convenient to contact.

Random sampling

A simple random sample involves selecting names randomly from a sampling frame. The most common ways of generating a random sample may be picking names out of a hat, or getting a computer to generate names. Using this technique, every member of the research population has an equal chance of being included in the sample, so those chosen are likely to be a cross section of the population. However, a simple random sample may not guarantee a representative sample — the technique may select too many young people or too many males, for example.

Systematic sampling

This involves a system for selecting names, such as every tenth name or every fourth name on your sampling frame. This does not always guarantee a representative sample, but the larger the sample, the more likely it is to be representative. This technique may be particularly useful if the sampling frame is in the form of a written list.

Stratified sampling (often referred to as stratified random sampling)

This technique is the most common and representative form of random sampling used in sociological research. It involves dividing the sampling frame into a number of sections or 'strata'. For example, if researchers were sampling students at a college and discovered that 60% of students were female and 40% were male, they would want their sample to reflect those proportions. The sampling frame, i.e. college registers, would need to be split into two: a list of female students and a list of male students. If the researchers intended to have an overall sample of 100 students, they could then randomly select 60 female and 40 male students from their two lists.

Knowledge check 9
Give one advantage and one disadvantage of choosing to use a stratified sample for your research.

Content Guidance

Non-random sampling techniques

Non-random sampling techniques may be used instead of random techniques for both practical and theoretical reasons. Sometimes no suitable sampling frame is available to the research team. For example, there is unlikely to be a sampling frame that lists the names of homeless people. Some interpretivists do not see the need for random sampling because they are interested in the specific experience of particular small-scale groups located in specific locations, for example homeless people who use a particular hostel. They have no intention of generalising their findings more widely, so a representative sample is not so important to them.

Snowball sampling

This type of sampling is used mainly when it is difficult to gain access to a particular group of people because there is no sampling frame available or because they engage in deviant or illegal activities that are normally carried out in isolation or in secret. The technique involves finding and interviewing a person who fits the research needs and then asking them to suggest another person who might be willing to be interviewed. The sample can grow as large as the researcher wants. However, snowball sampling may produce an atypical sample because those who agree to take part are unlikely to be representative of the wider group to which they belong, and will all be connected.

Volunteer sampling

People may be asked to volunteer to take part in research where the research question is too specific or even embarrassing for a wider audience and therefore results in a high level of non-response or refusal. To access volunteers, an advertisement could be placed on a website or in a newspaper, or a poster may be put up, for example. However, this is regarded as the weakest form of sampling since the volunteers are 'self-selecting' — choosing to take part for their own reasons and perhaps with strong views on the topic, affecting representativeness.

Opportunity sampling

Opportunity sampling involves researchers choosing individuals who are available at the time of the study. For example, if you wanted to research the views of students, you might just ask those who are free at the same time as you and easy to access.

Purposive sampling

Purposive sampling is when a researcher chooses specific people within the population to use for a particular study or research project. Usually, the researcher is not interested in a diverse research population. Rather they will want to focus on people with particular characteristics who will be better able to assist with the relevant research. For example, research on single mothers who are claiming benefits logically would look to sample precisely that group rather than mothers in general or single mothers who are not claiming benefits because they would be unable to relate anything relevant to the study. To access a purposive sample, the researcher will often go to a place where such people are likely to be found. For example, a researcher interested in how skateboarders see themselves might visit a local skate park over a weekend and ask all those present to take part in the research.

Quota sampling

This technique is often used by researchers from large-scale companies who do not have a sampling frame and select their sample by going to a public place such as a

Knowledge check 10

Which of the non-random sampling techniques is likely to achieve the most representative sample and why?

Exam tip

It is important to understand that sampling is a technique that helps sociologists to recruit people to take part in their research. Do not make the mistake of referring to sampling as a research method.

shopping centre or by going door to door and asking people they come across to take part. What makes it different from an opportunity sample is that such researchers are given quotas for different categories of people to fulfil. For example, they may have a quota of 30 males and 30 females and, within that, more specific quotas for different age groups. Once they have filled a particular quota, they will not ask any more of that type of person.

Access and gatekeeping

Researchers need to think carefully about how they are going to access the institution in which their research group is mostly likely to be found. Access to some groups may be relatively straightforward. For example, if the research is focused on teenagers, this group is most likely to be found in a school. Researchers could gain access to this group by writing to local education authorities and head teachers for permission.

Other groups may be quite difficult to access. For example, there is no sampling frame for elderly people and the researcher may be forced to use non-random methods such as purposive sampling at social events for older people, or snowball sampling asking any older contacts they have to access others.

Some sociologists have accessed particular groups via the internet, for example through chat rooms or interactive sites such as Facebook. This is especially useful for research situations that are potentially embarrassing and off-putting if carried out face to face. Some researchers have even set up interactive research sites where they post notices asking for volunteers, or questionnaires for internet users to complete.

Some groups have the power to deny access to sociologists. This is probably the main reason why there are few sociological studies of institutions such as private schools or big businesses. The person who has the power to grant access, and also potentially to control the sample used, is known as the **gatekeeper**. For example, if you wanted to study students in a college, the principal of the college would be the gatekeeper, and they could deny or grant you access. They could also decide to select the students for you, rather than allowing you to select your own representative sample. This could impact on representativeness, and thus the later generalisability of any research findings.

If a sociologist wants to access a group using participant observation they will usually need to share the social characteristics of the group. However, some groups do not want to be studied because they are engaged in deviant or criminal activity, so unless the researcher was covert and presented themselves as a group member, access could be difficult. Some sociologists have managed to access deviant or criminal worlds as participant observers by offering a service to the group or its leader or by being sponsored by a trusted member of the group, who reassures the group of the legitimacy of the newcomer and that they pose no threat to the group.

Ethics

The British Sociological Association argues that ethical issues are important because research can have a powerful impact on people's lives. It insists, therefore, that researchers must always think carefully about the impact of their research.

Gatekeeper A gatekeeper is a person who controls access to the group being studied. This may involve control over access to a sampling frame, or to specific participants, for example. In an observation context, the gatekeeper may be a member of a group that the researcher wishes to join, enabling an introduction.

Researchers need to acknowledge that research subjects have rights and that researchers have responsibilities and obligations towards them. There are certain broad ethical rules which underpin all sociological research, although some researchers will bend these rules and argue that the ends justify the means.

Informed consent

One issue is informed consent: research participants have a right to know what the research is about and the right to refuse to take part or to answer particular questions. People should know that research is being carried out on them and how the results will be used so that they can make an informed choice as to whether they should take part. Deception in any shape or form therefore needs to be avoided. However, informed consent is not always a straightforward matter. For example, very young children or people with learning disabilities may not be able to understand fully what the researcher is doing.

However, researchers using covert forms of observation depend on deception for the success of their research, and this would not be possible if their research subjects were informed that the research was taking place. This is because these groups tend to be involved in deviant behaviour and in normal circumstances would not be willing to cooperate with a sociological study. In these cases, interpretivists argue that deception is outweighed by the validity of the data gathered, which gives insight into why such deviance occurs.

Privacy and confidentiality

Another important issue is the right to privacy and confidentiality: most sociologists agree that the privacy of research subjects should be safeguarded as much as possible. However, sociological research is by its very nature intrusive — sociologists are interested in what goes on in private and intimate social situations. The problem of maintaining privacy can be countered by keeping the identity of research participants secret. Confidentiality means that the information an individual gives to the researcher cannot be traced back to that individual. Ethical researchers are therefore careful to disguise the identity of individual participants when they write up their research. If participants know they cannot be identified, they may be more willing to reveal personal and private matters, and thus confidentiality may increase the validity of the data collected.

Protection from harm

Most sociologists agree that research participants should be protected from any sort of physical harm and this is seldom a problem. However, some sociological research may harm participants emotionally and psychologically by asking insensitive questions or by reminding them of some traumatic experience. Sociological research may also have harmful social consequences. For example, people's reputations may be damaged or they may be exposed to ridicule because of something a sociologist has published.

Illegality and immorality

Sociologists should avoid being drawn into situations where they may commit crimes or assist/witness deviant acts. If they come into possession of information about crimes committed or about to be committed, for example, it is suggested that this should be reported to the relevant authorities. However, interpretivists argue that

> **Exam tip**
>
> When evaluating the usefulness of a research method to study a particular topic, consider whether ethical issues could constitute a strength and/or a weakness of such an approach.

> **Knowledge check 11**
>
> Explain how a 4-hour unstructured interview with a victim of domestic abuse could be seen as ethical, or unethical, from different perspectives.

if sociologists investigating deviant groups were to adopt this ethical rule, it would undermine the trust and rapport between the sociologist and research subjects and consequently seriously undermine the validity of the research. There are several famous studies which involve researchers going undercover into criminal gangs and finding themselves drawn into criminal behaviour.

Exploitation of research participants

Although it may appear that quantitative research such as questionnaires and structured interviews are less intrusive and thus less likely to create ethical issues, some researchers, especially feminists, have argued that another ethical concern involves the exploitation of research participants, arguing that more collaborative and in-depth research is actually more ethical as well, since the respondent has more control and gets more out of the experience. On the other hand, questionnaires tend to simply extract information from respondents, leaving them with nothing in return.

> **Summary**
>
> - The choice of research topic is influenced by a range of factors, including personal interest and which issues are current.
> - The research hypothesis and aims must be operationalised, that is, broken down into components such as indicators that can be measured and quantified.
> - The design and/or progress of a research project can be tested by using pilot studies or respondent validation.
> - Sociologists make a big contribution to social policy, but there is disagreement as to how involved sociologists should be with social policymakers.
> - It is usually impractical to study the whole of the population that sociologists are interested in and therefore some sociologists tend to use sampling frames and random sampling techniques in order to choose samples that are representative of the larger group.
> - If sampling frames are unavailable, sociologists might use non-random sampling techniques to gather suitable people to be researched.
> - There are various ethical guidelines that sociologists are expected to follow.

Which methods are used in sociological research?

Research methods

Questionnaires

Questionnaires are composed of standardised lists of questions that result from operationalising a hypothesis. They usually aim to gather a large quantity of research data, usually quantitative data, from large groups of people who may be situated in the same place or be geographically scattered. They are normally distributed by hand or through the post, although they are sometimes distributed through mass media publications such as newspapers and magazines or posted on websites.

Exam tip

Each of the following methods could be asked about in an exam question — you need to be comfortable with identifying and explaining at least three strengths and three weaknesses of each, in the research context given in the question/source.

Content Guidance

Questionnaire design can be a tricky business. The questions need to be asked in a clear and simple way and concepts fully operationalised, so that they are not misunderstood or misinterpreted by the research subjects, since there is no researcher to explain or clarify things. Questions must be free of bias — they must not lead respondents into giving the answers that support the hypothesis, nor should they be 'loaded' and/or provoke emotional responses that undermine validity because the research subject wants to evade either the truth or moral judgement about their behaviour. The questionnaire should be relatively short in order to avoid boring the research subject, who may not complete it or send it back if it seems like hard work. For this reason, open questions also tend to be avoided, since they take longer to complete. Most questionnaires use 'closed' questions. This is a question that is accompanied by limited range of answers, often in the form of tick boxes, such as true/false, or a range of options. Another form of closed question involves a statement with an attitudinal scale (for example, on a scale of 1–5, 1 being strongly agree and 5 being strongly disagree).

Strengths of questionnaires

Questionnaires have various strengths. They are useful for researching large numbers of people because they are cheap to design, print, distribute and analyse compared with other methods.

If an effective sampling frame exists, they can be sent through the post and therefore distributed to a geographically dispersed sample that can be compared for regional variations in behaviour and attitude. Thus, questionnaires are also more likely to generate representative samples because they can be sent out to thousands of people.

Questionnaires involve the minimum of contact with research subjects. The researcher is unlikely to be present when the respondent fills in the questionnaire and therefore unlikely to influence the results. For this reason, questionnaires may be useful for research into embarrassing, sensitive or deviant behaviour, especially if the researcher guarantees both anonymity and confidentiality. Moreover, people may prefer to answer questions on such topics in the privacy of their own homes rather than face to face with an interviewer.

According to positivists, questionnaires have the theoretical advantage of being an objective and value-free research tool which will produce a lot of quantitative data that can be compared and correlated. Questionnaires are also high in reliability, because they are standardised and therefore the procedure of distributing the questionnaire can be carried out many times and the results can be replicated and checked.

Weaknesses of questionnaires

A number of potential practical and theoretical problems have been identified with the questionnaire, especially the postal version.

The biggest practical problem is persuading people to return the questionnaire. This is less of a problem for those given out by hand because it is likely that the researcher will be waiting nearby to collect them in. However, it is a huge problem for postal questionnaires, which consequently suffer from poor **response rates**. This is likely to undermine the representativeness of the sample, and thus the generalisability of any findings. Furthermore, those who have responded are self-selecting and may be more likely to have a special interest in whatever is being researched, and are thus unrepresentative.

> **Exam tip**
>
> Make sure that you are able to identify theoretical as well as practical and ethical reasons why a sociologist uses a method like questionnaires or interviews. Ask yourself why a positivist or interpretivist might like or dislike this method.

> **Response rate** The proportion of people invited to take part in the research who actually complete it.

Another practical problem of questionnaires and the quantitative data that they generate is that a questionnaire is one-dimensional in its emphasis on closed questions. These may give sociologists information about patterns and trends, but it is difficult to go into any depth about motives or reasons for behaviour in a questionnaire because it needs to be kept short and simple. Some respondents may not cooperate with the research because they feel frustrated as the research design does not allow them to elaborate on their feelings and emotions.

Interpretivists criticise the use of questionnaires due to a lack of validity. For example, they argue that some people (especially those engaged in immoral, deviant or criminal behaviour) may associate questionnaires with authority (regardless of guarantees of anonymity). People may be less likely to respond to them, or if they do they may be less likely to give truthful responses because they feel threatened or frustrated by their inability to explain their answers. The closed questions will lead to a lack of depth: there is no way of knowing why people have ticked different boxes or what they meant by their answers. Interpretivists are therefore critical of questionnaires because they lack the means of looking inside people's heads — this is known as *verstehen* — and truly understanding their social reality.

> **Exam tip**
>
> Use concepts of validity and reliability to evaluate all research methods. If a method has high validity (and you need to explain why), it is likely to be low in reliability, and vice versa.

Structured interviews

A structured interview involves the researcher reading out questions from an interview schedule and writing down the respondent's answers. Such interviews allow little flexibility because the interviewer is not normally allowed to deviate from the questions on the interview schedule. Such interviews are popular with market researchers. The data collected are usually expressed in quantitative form because the questions are likely to be closed in nature.

Strengths of structured interviews

Many of the strengths of the structured interview are much the same as those of the questionnaire because the interview schedule is usually a set of closed questions using fixed-category answers and tick boxes — the only real difference is that the interviewer reads the questions out and fills the schedule in on behalf of the interviewee. Positivist sociologists, therefore, are keen on this research tool because, like the questionnaire, it has the scientific characteristics of reliability, objectivity and quantifiability.

Structured interviews can be carried out on relatively large samples because they can be conducted fairly quickly. They normally take anything between 10 and 30 minutes each to complete. However, the structured interview does have some advantages over the questionnaire, especially the postal version. Interviewers can ensure that the right person is answering the questions, which is impossible for researchers using the postal questionnaire, and can explain the aims and objectives and make sure the respondent is happy to participate. This may reduce potential non-response. An interviewee can also ask for clarification of questions they do not understand (although such questions should have been weeded out at the pilot stage).

Weaknesses of structured interviews

The structured interview experiences some of the same problems as the questionnaire because the interview schedule has been designed in much the same way.

Content Guidance

There is an additional problem of **interview bias**. For example, interviewees may react negatively to the social characteristics of the interviewer — their gender, ethnicity, age, perceived authority, accent and so on — and may not cooperate, or if they do they may engage in deception because they are anxious that the data might be used against them in some way.

There may also be a **social desirability** effect — this refers to the situation in which respondents work out from the research design what the researcher is looking for or they defer to interviewers and are eager to please them. The result of such interpretations is that interviewees may subconsciously change their behaviour to fit in with the research aims and give the researchers the replies they think the sociologist wants to hear. There is also a danger, present in all types of interview, that interviewers may unconsciously lead respondents into particular responses through their tone of voice or by their facial expression or body language.

Interpretivists are critical of structured interviews for much the same theoretical reasons that they are of questionnaires. They argue that the questions asked during such interviews are likely to be superficial and they fail to achieve *verstehen* — to achieve the sorts of qualitative data needed to understand how and why people interpret the world around them and behave the way they do.

Interpretivists also highlight the inflexibility of the structured interview. The robotic adherence to the interview schedule means that researchers rarely follow up interesting responses or ask why people behave in the way they do. Researchers do not have the time to build up the trust and rapport required to generate truly authentic data. Moreover, interpretivist sociologists point out that there is often a gap between what people say they do and what they actually do in practice. Many people are also unaware that they behave in the way they do.

Statistical data (official and non-official)

Official statistics

Official statistics are produced by government departments. The Office for National Statistics (ONS) gathers statistics that cover all aspects of economic and social life, such as work and unemployment, crime, births, deaths, marriage and divorce, health and education. For example, official crime statistics are produced from police figures and a national survey of victims that is carried out every year, and are a useful starting point for sociologists researching crime.

The government also employs social researchers to survey particular populations, usually to work out the efficacy of certain social policies. Every 10 years, the government carries out a survey on the whole population of the UK, using a questionnaire, which is called the Census. This provides a detailed snapshot of the population and its characteristics so that funding can be applied more effectively to public services. The last Census was carried out in 2011, the next will be in 2021.

Non-official statistics

These are the product of agencies outside of the government. For example, businesses, trade unions, political parties, pressure groups, think-tanks, and research organisations such as the Joseph Rowntree Foundation or the Sutton Trust, carry out research which results in statistical data relating to most aspects of social life.

Interview bias
Because an interview is a social exchange, bias may occur that impacts on the results and their validity. This may come from the interviewer and their expectations, and also from the interviewee, and the reactions to the interviewer and the situation.

Social desirability
This relates to the opinions, attributes and actions which are seen as ideal or more acceptable. People want to be viewed positively, and so are likely to give responses they think will achieve this, impacting on validity.

Strengths of official and non-official statistics

Official statistics are easy and cheap to access — they are often available via the internet and access to them therefore involves little effort or cost for the sociologist. Moreover, they are often up to date. This means that they also have a useful comparative value, since past statistical patterns can be compared with the present in order to establish trends or assess the success or failure of particular social policies.

Positivists value official statistics because they believe these data are collected in a scientific way, that is, the collection is standardised, reliable and objective. Government surveys also tend to use large representative and often national samples and therefore their findings can usually be generalised to similar populations.

Weaknesses of official and non-official statistics

Both official and non-official statistics can be problematic in terms of their use by sociologists, for several reasons. First, such statistics are not collected for sociological purposes. This may limit their usefulness because the definitions and concepts used by the government or non-official agencies may differ from those preferred by sociologists. For example, the definition of poverty used by the government or a right-wing think-tank may differ considerably from that used by those sociologists who believe that poverty is a massive social problem. One reason for this is that official and non-official agencies may not be as objective as positivists suggest. They often have a political agenda and consequently various biases may underpin any statistical data they produce. For example, a government may manipulate or massage statistics on unemployment, poverty and inequality in order to manage the electorate's impression of its policies as effective. Consequently, such statistics may not present a complete picture of what is going on. Trends may also lack validity, in that the methods of compiling statistics and definitions used may vary over time and between governments.

Interpretivists tend to be sceptical about the value of both official and non-official statistics, pointing out that such statistics are socially constructed. This means that they are the social product or end result of a powerful social group making a decision or judgement that a particular set of activities needs recording and that statistics need collecting. However, these decisions are sometimes selective and biased and consequently the statistics may say more about the powerful group that does the collecting than the social phenomena they are supposedly documenting or measuring. For example, the fact that black people are disproportionately represented in the official criminal statistics may be the product of police behaviour rather than black people being more criminal than other social groups. Interpretivists also argue that official and non-official statistics give little insight into the human stories behind them. For example, unemployment statistics do not tell sociologists anything about the everyday experience and humiliation of being unemployed.

Content analysis

Content analysis is usually a quantitative research method, which is used by sociologists to analyse media products such as advertisements, magazines, newspapers, websites, films, television news reports and even children's books and fairy tales. It involves counting the frequency of certain images, such as those contained in adverts and photographs, or words contained in newspaper/magazine articles or headlines.

> **Exam tip**
> When evaluating research methods in an exam question, make sure you consider the context of the research in the sources given in order to make your evaluation relevant and appropriate. For example, if statistics were used, where did the statistics come from and for what purpose may they have been collected orginally?

Content Guidance

Content analysis is normally based on a researcher constructing a content analysis schedule — this is a set of categories related to, for example, images and/or text that the researcher believes operationalises a research question or hypothesis. The researcher then samples the mass media product they are interested in and uses the content analysis schedule to 'observe', count and record how often the image and/or text occurs. In this way the qualitative content of the media is turned into quantitative data.

Content analysis can be conducted in a more in-depth way, which generates qualitative data. This would involve the researcher making a qualitative interpretation of the media content, perhaps describing the atmosphere or impressions it creates, or the underlying implications of the message. This approach is sometimes referred to as **semiology** and involves looking for signifiers and their connotations.

Semiology The study of signs and symbols, involving the interpretation of their meaning.

Strengths of content analysis

Content analysis is generally regarded as a cheap and easily accessible means of research. It is the best way of researching media content, which cannot be studied using questioning techniques.

Content analysis also allows the sociologist to compare mass media products or content over a period of time. For example, advertisements can be analysed from different time periods to work out whether their patriarchal content is increasing or decreasing. Positivists would regard quantitative content analysis as reliable because other sociologists can easily repeat and cross-check the results.

Weaknesses of content analysis

Quantitative content analysis has been criticised because counting media images or particular uses of text tells sociologists next to nothing about how those who use the media interpret or are affected by this content; it is just assumed that they are. At best, it can be argued that these images and text only give insight into the values and prejudices of those responsible for the social construction of media products, that is, journalists, editors, broadcasters, advertising executives and so on. Interpretivists would prefer a more semiological approach to content analysis, arguing that this will be higher in validity, although it may still not indicate the meaning that all members of the audience would perceive, only those of the researcher.

> **Exam tip**
>
> Note that content analysis is an unusual method because it combines the use of both primary and secondary data. The secondary data take the form of media reports that are analysed by the sociologist, therefore producing primary data. It is also the method that many students feel less clear about and often forget — so make sure you learn about it!

Ethnography

Ethnography is not a specific research method, but rather an approach to research. It literally means 'writing about a way of life'. Ethnographic research refers to any qualitative research project that is focused on providing a detailed and in-depth description of the everyday lives and practices of a group of people and that is as faithful as possible to the way those people see their lives themselves. Such a group may be large, as in the case of community studies of whole towns, or quite small, for example, an ethnographic study of a youth gang.

Ethnography is normally the preserve of interpretivists, who believe that researchers should focus on how people interact socially and how they interpret and construct their social reality. Interpretivists aim to 'get inside the heads' of the people they are studying so that they can see the world through their eyes. Ethnographic research often means long-term involvement in the everyday setting in which the research subjects are active. This may mean spending many months or even years in the places where the research subjects are to be found. The most common type of ethnographic research method is participant observation, which aims to develop an understanding of what it is like to live in a particular setting and to participate in the daily life of those being studied while observing it. Another type of ethnographic research is the unstructured interview.

Unstructured interviews

An unstructured interview is like a guided conversation, in that the interaction and talk between the sociologist and the interviewee are informal but the researcher plays an active yet subtle role in managing questions about the research topic to ensure that the interviewee remains focused on it. There will be few, if any, pre-set questions. The emphasis in these types of open-ended interviews is on spontaneity, flexibility and building trust. A successful unstructured interview is likely to be one in which the interviewee feels relaxed and unthreatened because the situation in which the questions are being asked feels natural. A skilled interviewer expertly and flexibly probes and follows up responses in such a sympathetic and empathetic way that the interviewee feels that a rapport has been established and they trust the interviewer so much that they are willing to volunteer richly detailed and qualitative information that they would not normally offer up in more formal research contexts.

Strengths of unstructured interviews

Interpretivists value this method for several reasons. The interview is likely to put the interviewee at ease, which means they are more likely to open up and say what they really feel and mean. In this sense, this type of interview is more likely to achieve *verstehen*, that is, to authentically see the world from the point of view of those being researched. If the subjects of the research can see that the researchers are genuinely interested in their experiences or are sympathetic to their situation, then they will be more willing to divulge and discuss sensitive issues and/or painful experiences that are unlikely to be revealed under other circumstances. Because of this, it can also be seen as an ethical method.

The spontaneity, flexibility and trust generated by such interviews mean that they produce highly valid data of first-hand accounts and interpretations of the issue that is being studied, often in the everyday speech of those being interviewed.

Weaknesses of unstructured interviews

Positivists are critical of unstructured interviews, however, because they allegedly are unscientific in that they lack reliability and objectivity. Positivists claim that they cannot be replicated because they are the product of the unique relationship that has been established between the interviewer and the interviewee. A different interviewer is therefore unlikely to achieve the same or similar results. Moreover, there is no standardised interview schedule that another sociologist could adopt to help repeat the research. Positivists also claim that such interviews and the data they generate are biased by the interviewers becoming too emotionally close to their interviewees and losing their objective detachment and neutrality.

Unstructured interviews are problematic for more practical reasons, in that they are often exceptionally time-consuming, expensive to conduct and transcribe, and

Content Guidance

the interviewing team's training needs to be thorough and specialised. For example, interviewers need to be trained in interpersonal skills in order to establish positive relationships with their interviewees.

The time-consuming nature of this method means that the number of those who participate as interviewees is likely to be small, affecting representativeness.

Semi-structured interviews

Semi-structured interviews, like unstructured interviews, consist of mostly open questions and generate qualitative data, therefore being preferred by interpretivists. The difference is that with semi-structured interviews there are some common open questions which will be asked to all respondents. Then, based on the answers, follow-up questions may be asked, making each interview unique. Semi-structured interviews, therefore, allow the interviewer to ask respondents for clarification of vague answers and to follow up and develop their responses. For example, the interviewer can jog a respondent's memory and ask them to give examples. These and other techniques can add depth and detail to responses and can help the sociologist to assess the participant's truthfulness.

Strengths and weaknesses of semi-structured interviews

Semi-structured interviews will have similar strengths to unstructured interviews, in terms of validity, rapport and *verstehen*, with the added strengths of being a little less time-consuming, since the common questions will prevent the interview from becoming too rambling, and of having more structure with some standardised questions, which improves reliability.

However, the same weaknesses also apply. Semi-structured interviews would be seen as lacking in objectivity and reliability by positivists, since every interview will be different.

Observations

Non-participant observation

Non-participant observation involves a non-participant observer simply watching and recording interaction and behaviour in a given situation such as a classroom or public place. Such an observer may be overt (open), for example, the presence of a stranger in a classroom will alert students to an observation, or covert (discreet/undercover), for example, the observer may be sitting in a café or bar but be recording people's behaviour without their knowledge. Some researchers may choose to observe a group or interaction via a CCTV camera or one-way mirror.

Non-participant observation normally involves the observer using an observation schedule made up of a set of categories of behaviour that they might be expected to see and that can be ticked off and quantified. The existence of an observation schedule means that this research method is reasonably reliable as it can be repeated by other researchers, although the schedule needs to be carefully operationalised so observers know exactly what they are looking for. Such observation thus generates quantitative data. However, it would be possible to conduct more qualitative, in-depth observations, for example by making notes describing the scenes witnessed, or by filming them in order to analyse the events in more detail.

> **Exam tip**
> Remember that semi-structured interviews are *not* a halfway house between structured and unstructured interviews, combining qualitative and quantitative data — this is a common mistake made by students. They will generally consist of open questions, and therefore will gain qualitative data and be favoured by interpretivists.

> **Exam tip**
> Be able to compare the advantages/weaknesses of the three different types of interview. Think too about variations on interviews, such as group interviews and focus groups.

Supporters of this type of observation argue that because the researcher is detached from the group and therefore objective, their interpretation of the group's behaviour is less likely to be biased. Moreover, because the researcher does not make any decisions or join in the group's activities, the group itself will not be influenced by the observer. However, critics point out that if the observer is visible then those being observed are likely to act unnaturally because they may feel anxious or threatened by the fact that the observation is taking place. If the observation is not supported by other methods such as interviews it is unlikely to provide much insight into why people behave in the way that they do.

Exam tip

In an exam question about observation, make sure you read the source carefully to work out whether it is using participant or non-participant observation and what kind of data it is gathering, as well as whether the observation is overt or covert, since this will affect the way in which you evaluate the use of the method.

Participant observation: overt and covert

Overt participant observation

Participant observation involves the observer immersing themselves in the lifestyle of the group being studied for weeks, months or even years. These sociologists participate in the same activities as the group being researched and observe their everyday lives. The aim is to understand what is happening from the point of view of those involved, to 'get inside their heads' and to understand the meaning that they ascribe to their situation.

Usually, the observer gains access to the group via a gatekeeper — someone who belongs to the group and who has the respect and trust of the others and is therefore able to gain their consent. This type of observation is sometimes supplemented with informal or unstructured interviews, that is, conversations that take place during the course of the observation. The observer will use these to cross-check with members of the group that what they are observing is shared by all members of the group, so increasing the validity of the data.

Participant observation involves 'hanging around' waiting for something to happen — in this sense, it is often misinterpreted and criticised as unstructured and unplanned. However, this is because the interpretivists who carry out this type of research generally go into it open-minded. They are willing to let their research aims develop organically as the research progresses because observation and conversation often eventually result in the observer learning the answers to questions they would not normally have asked if using questionnaires and interviews.

Covert participant observation

Sometimes it is impossible to find a gatekeeper, or the group is just not interested in being the subject of research because its members are engaged in illegal and/or deviant activities or are suspicious of conventional society, such as might be found with religious sects. Sometimes the researcher might simply believe that overt research is too likely to produce artificial behaviour in those being observed, especially if it is a group that is accountable, such as the police. In order to overcome these problems a researcher might decide to infiltrate the group covertly by taking on a different identity.

Content Guidance

This type of undercover observation takes considerable skill (and often courage) if it is to be successful because the person under cover needs to be a convincing actor and has to be constantly on guard against their cover being blown. They must find a way of recording information that is not going to arouse suspicion. Such research is very stressful because it involves constant vigilance in order not to lose the trust and confidence of the group, constant risk-taking and even physical danger.

Strengths of participant observation

Interpretivists are keen on this method because it achieves *verstehen* — the researcher sees things through the eyes of the group being studied because they are in the same situation as the group's members and they experience what they are experiencing. The sociologist therefore gains a first-hand insider's view through watching and listening, and uncovers the priorities, concerns, anxieties and motivations of the observed group. The observer will probably see things that are unlikely to be voluntarily revealed in an interview or on a questionnaire.

Observation — especially when it is covert — is high in validity because the researcher can see what people do in their natural setting as opposed to what they say they do when asked in questionnaires or interviews. Observation can also lead to unexpected findings that generate new insights into people's behaviour. Additionally, observers often engage in reflexivity and record all their interactions in a research diary to assess whether the behaviour they observe is the result of their presence, and then will sometimes discuss their observations with the group at a later point as a form of respondent validation.

Weaknesses of participant observation

Participant observation breaks a number of ethical rules. Covert observation in particular has been criticised for its deception. It is argued that it abuses the trust and friendship of people in the group who are being observed. Participant observation has also been criticised because some observers have taken part in illegal or unethical behaviour in order to gain or reinforce the trust of the group being researched.

Participant observation has been accused of not being objective. It is suggested that observers are often biased because they become too sympathetic towards those they are observing. It is claimed that it is too easy for observers to lose their detachment and 'go native'. The observer then interprets the behaviour of the group in a positive light, which allegedly biases their analysis of the group's actions.

Positivists stress the unreliability of participant observation. There is no way that the research can be repeated as a means of verifying its descriptions and conclusions. It is not possible to judge whether the social context or the people studied are representative, or whether the presence of the researcher changed the behaviour of the group more than was realised. Moreover, the success of the research is often due to the exclusive relationships they have constructed. Another sociologist might find it impossible to gain the same degree of trust and rapport with the observed group.

This type of research is also criticised for lacking generalisability because the observer cannot practically study large numbers of people or the wider context within which the research setting is located. Participant observation also has a number of practical problems. It is time-consuming and expensive.

> **Exam tip**
>
> Be specific when answering questions on observation, as there are different types. Be guided by the question but also by the type of observation used in the source material.

Mixed methods

Many sociologists use a combination of research methods, often aiming to gain both quantitative and qualitative data, rather than confining themselves to one method. There are two approaches to mixing methods.

Triangulation

Triangulation is usually adopted so that the sociologist is able to get a better view of the overall picture of what they are studying by looking at it from a number of different angles. It normally involves combining methods that result in quantitative and qualitative data in order to check and verify the validity and reliability of the data collected by each method. For example, a sociologist using participant observation might check the reliability of their findings by conducting a follow-up questionnaire. Similarly, a researcher who has carried out structured interviews may then ask some of the respondents to take part in an unstructured interview to gain more depth and validity in relation to their answers. Qualitative research may also produce hypotheses that can be checked using statistical methods — for example, participant observation might produce unexpected behaviour that could be further investigated using a questionnaire survey.

Methodological pluralism

Methodological pluralism combines research methods in order to build up a fuller picture of what is being studied. For example, a researcher might begin their research by looking at official statistics relating to the behaviour they are investigating. They might then proceed to conduct a questionnaire using large samples of people scattered across the country in order to test whether the behavioural trends seen in the official statistics have changed. Finally, in order to elicit qualitative data about why people behave in the way they do, a small sample of people might be invited to take part in in-depth unstructured interviews. Some sociologists reject the divide between scientific positivists and quantitative data on the one hand, and the more micro interpretivists' approach on the other, and prefer to get a broader picture.

Problems with using mixed methods

Some problems have been identified with the use of mixed methods. They are often time-consuming and expensive and produce vast amounts of data, which can be difficult to analyse. Priority tends to be given to one method at the expense of the others — they rarely have equal status. This is because survey researchers do not have the same skills as ethnographers and vice versa. Additionally, mixed methods can sometimes produce contradictory findings. This poses a problem in terms of what should be kept and what should be discarded.

Exam tip

If you are asked to evaluate the use of mixed methods, you can consider the strengths and weaknesses of the methods individually, but you MUST make sure you also focus on the good and bad points about using BOTH methods together.

Content Guidance

> **Summary**
>
> - There are several research methods used by sociologists, and which one(s) are used will depend on the theoretical approach adopted and the topic being investigated, as well as on practical and ethical considerations.
> - Questionnaires are one of the most popular research methods, but despite their advantage in hitting large numbers of people, they can be one-dimensional and superficial in terms of the data collected.
> - Structured interviews also gather large amounts of quantitative data, via mainly closed questions, but the validity of the data collected can be undermined by the lack of depth and the interaction between the interviewer and the interviewee.
> - Interviews can also be semi-structured or unstructured. Semi- and unstructured interviews tend to comprise open questions and generate qualitative data.
> - A cheap source of quantitative data is statistical data collected by official agencies, such as government departments, although sociologists need to be careful when using these data because they are not collected for sociological reasons.
> - Another way of interpreting more qualitative secondary data is to use content analysis, a systematic technique often used to categorise media content.
> - Some sociologists prefer to immerse themselves in the everyday lives of those being studied in order to produce data high in validity and therefore adopt ethnographic methods such as participant observation, which involves establishing relationships with those being studied.
> - Many sociologists use a mixture of methods in order to generate both quantitative and qualitative data. This can be to maximise both reliability and validity, through triangulation, or to gain a wider perspective through methodological pluralism.

Section B Understanding social inequalities

The following two key questions are applied to four aspects of inequality: social class, gender, ethnicity and age.

1. **What are the main patterns and trends in social inequality and difference?**

   For each of the above four aspects of inequality you need to know evidence of patterns and trends in social inequality and difference from a range of areas of social life, which must include the workplace. Evidence relating to workplace inequality is provided for each aspect below. For some areas, such as social class and old age, evidence on health inequalities is also provided, since it may prove particularly useful and relevant. You should also include evidence from other areas of the specification you have studied, such as education, crime, family, media, religion or youth subcultures.

2. **How can patterns and trends in social inequality and difference be explained?**

   You also need to understand how the different theories have explained each aspect of inequality. You need to apply the following theories: functionalism, the New Right, Marxism, Weberian views and feminism.

Social inequality and social class

Evidence relating to social class inequalities

Workplace

One issue relating to workplace inequality is inequality of access to top jobs. Evidence from the Sutton Trust links the top professions such as judges to attending private schools and Oxbridge/Russell Group universities.

UK income inequality has increased in the last 40 years, particularly in the 1980s, but also in recent years since the 2009 recession. High Pay Centre figures for 2018 show that the median annual pay of chief executives of the 100 largest companies was £4.85 million, (even with two extremely high pay figures excluded), which is 145 times the average pay of their employees. This pay gap is increasing every year.

Occupations held by the working class usually have lower pay and status, fewer in-work benefits and promotion prospects, and less job security than middle-class occupations. Around 5 million British people are paid at a level below the 'real' living wage (which, in 2019, should be £9.30 per hour, as calculated by the Living Wage Foundation, based on living costs). Wadsworth (2007) points out that many minimum wage earners take a second job to supplement income.

Social Mobility Commission research (2017) found an average class pay gap of 17% for those in the same job, based on class background. Even when professionals had the same educational attainment, role and experience, those from poorer families

> **Exam tip**
> You could be asked specifically about workplace inequalities for social class, gender, ethnicity or age. However, you could also have a general question on inequalities or relative advantages/disadvantages in society. It is a good idea to learn evidence for at least two other areas, as well as workplace, for each aspect of inequality.

> **Exam tip**
> Other theories, such as interactionism and postmodernism, may provide useful ideas which can be used as evaluation or in a more general question, but you would not get a question focusing specifically on these.

> **Knowledge check 12**
> Explain what is meant by the 'class pay gap'.

Content Guidance

were paid an average of £2,242 less per year. The odds of those from professional backgrounds ending up in professional jobs are 2.5 times higher than those from less advantaged backgrounds.

Health

Working-class people experience poorer mortality and morbidity rates than the middle class. Over 3,500 more working-class babies would survive per year if the working-class infant mortality rate was reduced to middle-class levels. Wilkinson and Pickett (2014) found that working-class people are more likely to die before retirement of cancer, stroke and heart disease than middle-class people. In London, there is a 25-year life expectancy gap between the rich and the poor.

Bann et al. (2017) showed that socioeconomic disadvantage in childhood is associated with higher body mass index (BMI) that persists with age and over different generations. This also has an effect on other health issues, including diabetes and heart disease.

In 2018 food banks were used by almost 4 million people in the UK. Wakeman's research (2015) suggested that families who rely on food banks may suffer nutritional deficiencies because so much of the produce is processed rather than fresh.

Explanations for social class inequality

Functionalist explanations

Functionalists argue that stratification and inequality perform a positive function for society. However, they generally do not accept that there are inequalities of opportunity — just unequal outcomes.

Durkheim (1893) argued that in a complex industrial society, the division of labour is functional — people should specialise and occupations should be graded in terms of their value to society and rewarded accordingly. Thus, a stratified system (with different levels) is functional since it sets limits on people's aspirations but still offers incentives to work harder.

Parsons (1951) developed these ideas, also arguing that social stratification is inevitable, functional and fair. Parsons believed that society is **meritocratic** — especially through the education system.

Incentives and competition ensure that talented people work hard and succeed, and education socialises us into these ideas and also allocates us to appropriate roles, based on merit — referred to as 'role allocation'.

Similar ideas were put forward by Davis and Moore (1945), who discussed how education 'sifts and sorts' individuals into appropriate roles. The function of social institutions such as education is to allocate all individuals to an occupational role that suits their abilities (role allocation) via examinations and qualifications. If societies are to operate effectively, they have to ensure that their most functionally important and senior positions are filled by people who are talented and efficient, hence the need to pay higher salaries to those senior roles.

Thus role allocation produces stratification in the form of economic and social inequality — because not all people are equally talented or skilled. Moreover,

---

Exam tip

Expand the range of points you have in relation to workplace by linking in points relating to educational achievement and access, for example. Also consider applying concepts you have used elsewhere in the course, such as the old boy network, and cultural and social capital.

Exam tip

For a 20-mark question relating to evidence for inequality, aim to cover different areas (such as work, education, crime, health etc.) and include at least four points relating to inequality, well explained and supported by evidence, in total. Remember you are not explaining these inequalities, so focus on evidence (such as statistics or other research findings, studies and concepts) rather than applying theories.

Meritocracy A system where talent and effort will equal reward, so people get what they deserve.

Knowledge check 13

Give examples to show how education may socialise us to accept that society is meritocratic.

inequality is further increased by the fact that those in the top jobs are paid significantly higher salaries than those in other jobs. This inequality results in the emergence of different social classes.

Members of society who lack the qualities required for top jobs and who therefore occupy relatively low positions in the stratification system uncritically accept their social position. This is because they have been successfully socialised into agreeing that some jobs deserve higher rewards than others because they are functionally more important to the smooth running of society. As a result, people are generally happy to accept that surgeons deserve more economic rewards than hospital porters, for example. This **value consensus** also means that most members of society believe that their own social class position is a fair reflection of their talent and ability. Consequently, functionalists believe that stratification is necessary and beneficial because it encourages all members of society to work to the best of their ability — those at the top will work hard to retain their advantages, while those below are motivated to work hard to improve themselves.

Evaluation of functionalist explanations

Functionalists may have exaggerated the degree of consensus about rewards. There is some resentment in UK society with regard to the salaries earned by groups such as bankers and business leaders, especially as other occupational groups have been subjected to austerity measures in the form of pay freezes or below-inflation wage growth.

Unequal rewards may be the product of the power of some groups to increase their rewards regardless of so-called consensus. For example, the pay of company directors is set by them, not by society.

The top of the stratification system is occupied not only by those with functionally important jobs but also by those who live off inherited wealth and by celebrities. Neither of these latter groups is necessarily functionally important to society.

Evidence suggests that not all those who occupy top jobs are the most talented. Family connections, the ability to pay for exclusive and expensive private education, the old boy network, and hidden forms of institutional patriarchy and racism, rather than talent or ability, may have propelled the children of the white wealthy elite to the top.

There are many occupations that are not highly rewarded that can be seen as functionally essential to the smooth running of society, such as nursing, water and sewage work, and refuse collection.

Functionalists also neglect the dysfunctions of stratification, such as poverty, which negatively impacts on people and their mortality, health, education, standard of living and so on. Crime, riots and lack of community may be other dysfunctions of social class inequality.

New Right explanations

New Right thinker Charles Murray blames inequalities in outcomes on the inadequate norms and values of those at the bottom of the social structure — the **underclass** — thus supporting functionalist ideas of meritocracy. In 1989, Murray wrote: 'There are many ways to identify an underclass. I will concentrate on three

Value consensus This refers to the idea that there is general agreement in society about what is important and the key goals for which everyone will strive, such as hard work, success and so on.

Exam tip

Remember that evaluation can take two forms in any essay: you can develop specific criticism of the theory and its explanations, but you can also use the ideas of opposing theories to challenge the theory in question.

Underclass This term refers to those at the bottom of the class structure, such as the long-term unemployed, who are thus not part of the 'working class'. The term is controversial in the way it has been used by the New Right to imply a judgement about its members, involving a perceived lack of work ethic and a dependency culture, which other sociologists would challenge.

Content Guidance

phenomena that have turned out to be early-warning signals in the United States: illegitimacy, violent crime, and drop-out from the labour force.'

Murray sees these three factors as connected to overgenerous benefits, allowing single-parent (usually female-led) families to survive, and leading to a generation of unruly young males who lack male role models and discipline. His ideas were developed in relation to the USA, and largely directed at minority ethnic groups, but he came to Britain in the early 1990s and said they also applied in the UK, influencing the Conservative government's policies on welfare and single parents. Thus, his explanation for social class inequality lies with the culture and choices of those at the bottom of the class structure, encouraged by a welfare system which rewards irresponsible behaviour and undermines the important link between actions and consequences. Murray's solution to poverty is to drastically reduce or cut benefits altogether, which would ultimately discourage or prevent those with a poor work ethic and lower intelligence from reproducing.

British New Right thinker Saunders (1990) agrees with Murray, suggesting that there is a lower layer of people in British society who are poor, unqualified and unemployed and who tend to share characteristics including multiple deprivation (financial, social and educational), dependence on state welfare provision and a culture of fatalism — thus suggesting that an attitude and set of behaviours demonstrated by such people actually contributes to their position. Saunders suggests that achievement in society is mainly based on merit, thus people get what they deserve.

Saunders also argues that social inequality is the price to be paid for the fact that economic growth has raised the living standards of the majority of people in the UK and other Western nations. Saunders points out that even the poor are much better off today than they were in the past. He argues that capitalist societies have to offer incentives to those with talent and enterprise in the form of more income and wealth because these people are the innovators — the only ones capable of catching the public imagination with a constant stream of in-demand consumer goods such as smartphones and social media such as Facebook and Instagram. If these material incentives did not exist, talented people would not have been motivated to produce the consumer goods society takes for granted. In this sense, class stratification and the inequality that it produces is a necessary by-product of society's demand for the latest consumer innovations.

Evaluation of New Right explanations

New Right ideas have been widely criticised. They involve moral judgements about 'acceptable' values and generalise about those who do not conform, based on the assumption that everyone has equal opportunities and the freedom to make choices. This would be challenged by Marxists for not recognising the structural disadvantages faced by those at the bottom.

Some have used evidence to counter Murray's claims. For example, Walker (1990) showed that at least 50% of those born in a disadvantaged home did not end up disadvantaged themselves, challenging the idea that parents pass on a fatalistic attitude and work ethic. Additionally, Walker showed that 60% of illegitimate births to women under 20 were registered to both parents, and suggested that lone parenthood is often short lived (less than 3 years). He argues that most members

Knowledge check 14

Identify two key similarities between the functionalist and New Right views of class inequality.

Exam tip

Use functionalism and the New Right to support each other as a way of adding additional range to an essay on either of these views.

of the underclass have conventional norms and values, in that they want stable relationships and paid employment. It is lack of opportunities which prevents them from achieving these aims.

Heath's (1990) data also cast doubt on Murray's claim that those in the underclass have different attitudes. Of the people on benefits, 80% said they would like to have a paid job, compared to only 57% of people from families where at least one person was working, challenging the idea that those on benefits are not willing to work.

Young (2003) also condemns the picture presented by the New Right, as a 'sociology of vindictiveness' that seeks to 'punish, demean and humiliate' those at the bottom of society. He argues that certain sections of society, such as teenage mothers, beggars and immigrants, are portrayed as contributing to the problems of society disproportionally to their actual impact. Young suggests that these groups are an 'easy enemy' and become scapegoats, rather than being seen as the victims of an unfair system.

Marxist explanations

Marx argued that capitalist societies are stratified by social class, which is the product of the infrastructure/mode of production or economic 'base' of a society. Modern capitalist societies have an industrial factory-based infrastructure in which companies compete to sell manufactured goods.

Marx argued that the infrastructure was based on two components:

- the **means of production**, which are owned by a minority group: the capitalist class or bourgeoisie
- the social relations of production — which refers to the relationship between the bourgeoisie and the working class or proletariat, in which the latter hire out to the former, in exchange for a wage, their labour power

Class inequalities in wealth, income and power are rooted in the capitalist infrastructure because it is in the interests of the capitalist class to keep wages low in order to increase profits. Moreover, the capitalist class exploits the labour power of the proletariat by controlling the organisation of work — for example, by controlling the speed of assembly lines — and by appropriating the **surplus value** of the worker's labour power. Marxists, therefore, believe that class stratification and inequality are caused by the exploitation of workers by the bourgeoisie.

Marx also focused on why workers are not often aware of class exploitation. He argued that workers experience **false consciousness**. They have been fooled by another important component of capitalism, the **superstructure**, which is made up of institutions such as education and religion, into believing that the class stratification found in capitalist societies is fair and natural.

Neo-Marxists developed these ideas, arguing that the function of the superstructure is the reproduction and legitimisation of class inequality through the transmission of ruling-class ideology. Althusser (1970) describes the institutions of the superstructure as 'state apparatus'.

- The repressive state apparatus (RSA) — which includes the government and the legal and criminal justice systems — directly and obviously controls the proletariat.

Means of production
Resources, such as land, factories, machinery and raw materials, which are owned by the bourgeoisie or capitalist class.

Surplus value
The difference between the value produced by the labour power of the worker and the wage paid to the worker. This difference is pocketed by the bourgeoisie in the form of profit.

False consciousness
The mistaken awareness experienced by the proletariat, that the inequalities in society are fair and natural, which is created and reinforced by the superstructure.

Superstructure
The institutions built onto the economic base of a society that are shaped by, but also reinforce, that base. In capitalist societies, the superstructure, including institutions such as the family, religion, education and the media, reinforces the values of capitalism.

Content Guidance

- The ideological state apparatuses (ISAs) — including the media and education — control us by socialising us into accepting the capitalist ideology, thus creating false consciousness. This ideological control is key to the maintenance of power by the capitalist class, since no 'class can hold power over a long period without exercising ideological control', according to Althusser.

Bowles and Gintis (1976) agree, describing the 'myth of meritocracy' promoted by the education system in capitalist societies. The function of education is to legitimise the success of bourgeois children while working-class children are taught by schools to accept academic failure and develop the qualities required by the capitalist system, such as obedience and respect.

Bourdieu (1984) suggests that the children of the upper and middle classes are ensured educational and economic success because they have **cultural capital** — that is, the values and attitudes that teachers embrace — and economic advantages, for example, their parents can afford private education. Working-class children, meanwhile, lack cultural capital and are condemned to a life of manual work due to achieving few qualifications. Nevertheless, they rarely blame the capitalist system for their 'failure' because the ideology of meritocracy ensures that they blame themselves. The organisation of capitalism, therefore, is rarely challenged and class stratification and inequality are reproduced generation after generation.

Cultural capital This consists of values, beliefs, knowledge and language skills that benefit children in educational environments.

Evaluation of Marxist explanations

Marxism has been accused of economic reductionism. This means that Marxists see all inequality as the product of the economic relationship between the bourgeoisie and the proletariat. However, other theories such as Weberian and feminist approaches suggest that inequalities and conflicts relating to gender, ethnicity and age cannot be adequately explained in exclusively economic terms.

Marx did not anticipate the rise of the middle classes and consequently their role in the stratification system. Thus, although his prediction that the top and bottom classes would polarise and the gap between them would grow was generally right, the growth of those in the middle has undermined his expectations that class consciousness would develop.

Despite Marxist ideas relating to false consciousness, evidence suggests that many workers *are* aware of social class inequalities. Some have taken up the political fight against them, while others believe that such inequalities are a lesser evil compared with the standard of living that capitalism has provided them with. The working class may be consciously reconciled to capitalism rather than falsely conscious or ignorant of how it produces inequality.

> **Exam tip**
>
> If you are faced with a question that focuses on 'functionalist' or 'Marxist' explanations of inequality, you could evaluate the theory using the opposing view. Remember not to merely juxtapose these views, though. Use the other theory to directly challenge the view in the question, showing how and why they disagree.

Weberian explanations

Weber was writing after Marx and Durkheim, but was very much influenced by Marx's ideas, although he disagreed with him in many ways. Weber argued that there are three main sources of power in society: class, status and party.

Weber saw class in a qualitatively different way to Marx, in that he defined it in terms of market position — for example, people's skills, qualifications, control over the work process, and income — thus recognising different class groupings, based on market position, as well as relationship to the means of production. This led to

Section B Understanding social inequalities

Weber pointing out that within broad social classes there exist groups that differ in status from each other. For example, some members of the working class are skilled workers — they are likely to have completed training and qualifications and consequently they are paid reasonably well. These skilled workers therefore have a better market position than semi-skilled, unskilled and unemployed members of the working class, which means they enjoy superior incomes and lifestyles. Weber also thought that the middle class contained different levels, and that it would continue to grow and diversify. This is a key distinction between his and Marx's ideas, in which Weber has proved the more accurate.

Status refers to the social standing of a group — how society ranks groups in terms of prestige and importance. Weber agreed with Marx that status could be shaped by social class, but he also identified a number of other sources of status which he believed were just as important in bringing about stratification and inequality. For example, in some societies, people may be regarded as having low status because of their skin colour and/or because they belong to a minority ethnic group that is the victim of racism. Many societies are patriarchal, judging females as having low status. Consequently, women do not enjoy the same power and privileges as males. Additionally, status could come from your family background, your job or your lifestyle. Status could also come from consumption: how you choose to spend your money and present yourself. Purchasing 'status symbols', such as designer clothes or a flashy car, could gain you status in the eyes of others.

A third aspect of inequality identified by Weber was party. By party, Weber was referring to the power which can be gained through membership of certain groups. 'Parties' in this sense can include a whole range of things, from membership of a powerful family, attendance at a prestigious school or university, to membership of a political party, trade union or association. Such 'parties' possess different levels of influence, and can give their members advantages. For example, an 'old Etonian' may find certain job opportunities open up for him via the old boy network.

More recent sociologists influenced by Weber's ideas have particularly picked up on the class and status aspects of his analysis. Goldthorpe et al. (2007) were responsible for developing the current scale used by the government to assess class — the National Statistics Socio-economic Classification or NS-SEC. This measure of class includes assessing how 'routine' a person's occupation is, as well as the marketable skills involved, moving away from the previous manual/non-manual split. In this way, Weberian ideas relating to market position, status and the growth of and fragmentation of the middle class are widely accepted.

Another Weberian view comes from Parkin (1968), who looked at the different tactics classes use to defend or improve their position — exclusion (of those lower than you) and usurpation (of those above you). The middle class have to use both these tactics as they try to usurp the upper class above them, but also exclude the working class from climbing to their level. This links to the concept of **social closure**, which was alluded to by Weber when he discussed 'open and closed social relations' and the different degrees and motivations for closure to benefit a group.

The **dual labour market theory** (Barron and Norris 1976) also demonstrates Weberian ideas of status in its view of class and occupation — occupations in the secondary labour market have lower status, less job security and fewer rights than

> **Knowledge check 15**
> Which more current theory would agree with Weberian ideas about individuals gaining status through consumption?

Social closure The way in which a social group (such as a class, gender or ethnic group) maintains its power and monopoly over resources via the exclusion of others from the group.

Dual labour market theory This suggests dividing occupations into two categories: primary sector jobs that are high status, salaried and permanent, with good career prospects; and secondary sector jobs that are often temporary and/or part-time, low status, paid by the hour at low rates and lacking job security or benefits. Secondary sector jobs are more likely to be held by women, people in lower social classes, certain minority ethnic groups and younger workers.

Researching and understanding social inequalities

Content Guidance

the primary labour market (middle class). This view is explored further in the ethnicity and gender sections below.

Evaluation of Weberian explanations

The Weberian focus on status may explain the divisions that exist within social classes between both middle-class and working-class workers and between male and female white workers and workers from different ethnicities. However, the Weberian analysis has been criticised by Marxists for neglecting what they see as the most important exploitative relationship between capitalists and workers. Marxists argue that class and status are strongly linked because the capitalist class has status and power since it monopolises wealth and income. However, while Weber recognised that these factors overlap, he noted that a person can have a lot of wealth but little status (for example, a lottery winner) or high status but very little wealth (for example, a religious leader).

Feminist explanations

Most feminists focus their explanations of inequality on gender. However, Marxists feminists do discuss the intersection of gender and social class, and how women and working-class men both suffer exploitation, and so their ideas could be applied to explaining social class inequalities.

Marxist feminists such as Beechey (1979) contend that women are additionally oppressed within the labour market, and also used to further contribute to male workers' oppression by being seen as part of a **reserve army of labour**. The ability to fill in gaps in the labour market with low-paid and often part-time appointments serves to undermine the security and employment rights of the main labour force, while those in the reserve army experience particularly low levels of pay and job security. Women have historically been used in this capacity, for example during the Second World War — brought in to fill in for the men who were fighting but then pushed out again on their return. The rise of the so-called '**gig economy**' in recent years, with many temporary and part-time jobs, in particular 'zero-hours contracts', illustrates the continued importance of the reserve army of labour to capitalist economy, and women continue to form a significant part of this.

Margaret Benston (1972) argues that a wife keeps her husband in good running order by feeding and caring for him and that this is essential to the smooth running of capitalism. In addition, the fact that a man must provide for his wife and children means that he is less likely to challenge the capitalist system, thus maintaining class inequality. Benston believes that the unpaid domestic labour of women helps support the capitalist system and thus social class inequality. She contends that if women were paid a wage for their work in the home, there would have to be a massive redistribution of wealth.

From this perspective, dual systems theorists such as Hartmann (1979) and Mitchell (1971) argue that capitalism benefits from compliant women, who have been socialised to accept their place in society and to rear their children — the next generation of workers — in the same way. Women are involved in the **social reproduction of labour power**, both by producing children and by passing on the capitalist ideology they were reared to accept. Thus, the dual systems of capitalism and patriarchy combine to oppress women for the benefit of the bourgeoisie.

Reserve army of labour Workers who are brought in and also pushed out of the labour market as conditions dictate.

Gig economy A labour market characterised by short-term and/or zero-hours contracts or freelance work as opposed to permanent jobs.

The social reproduction of labour power The rearing of the next generation of workers, usually taking place within the family. This would include feeding, clothing and socialising children, bringing them up to replace previous generations of workers to ensure that capitalism can continue to thrive.

Section B Understanding social inequalities

According to Ansley (1976), another role women play in support of capitalism is to soothe the stresses and frustrations of proletariat men after a hard day at work. In this sense women act as 'safety valves' for men, as husbands return home having been exploited at work and take out their pent-up emotions on their wives rather than on their employees. She contends that, 'When wives play their traditional role as takers of shit, they often absorb their husbands' legitimate anger and frustration at their own powerlessness and oppression. With every worker provided with a sponge to soak up his possibly revolutionary ire, the bosses rest more secure.'

Ansley, therefore, demonstrates the important role that women play in maintaining capitalism and social class inequality.

Evaluation of feminist explanations

Writers such as Hakim argue that feminists underestimate women's choice — many women choose to work in a part-time or flexible way and would not see this as a form of exploitation. The reserve army of labour argument also neglects issues of horizontal segregation and the gender pay gap, by focusing only on employment or unemployment.

Arguments about unpaid domestic labour are also contentious. Many would argue that such labour is a private matter relating to one's own family rather than serving the needs of capitalism or contributing to class inequality.

Another objection to ideas such as paying a wage for housework, which has been promoted by some Marxist feminists, is that it is outdated now, in that most women do not solely focus on the housewife role and are in fully paid work, and that many males now contribute equally to domestic tasks in dual-career families. To promote paid housework for women would take their role back decades.

> **Exam tip**
>
> There is more on Marxist feminism in the gender section below. You can use Marxist feminists for Marxist views on gender inequality as well as for feminist views on class inequality.

Summary: social class inequality

- Inequalities in society, including in educational and employment opportunities and in health, undermine the life chances of those in the working class.
- Functionalists and the New Right focus on inequality of outcomes, rather than inequality of opportunities, arguing that UK society is meritocratic and that unequal outcomes are thus fair and functional.
- Marxists focus on the class struggle between the bourgeoisie (or owners of the means of production) and the proletariat (or workers). Social class inequality is created by and benefits the bourgeoisie, and is maintained through the exploitation of the proletariat and the institutions which keep them in a state of false consciousness.
- Weberians see social class inequality as more complex than Marxists, bringing in the additional dimensions of status and party, and seeing class as based on market position.
- Feminists, especially Marxist feminists, recognise the role of capitalism and the social class inequality in its particular oppression of women, through their unpaid and low-paid labour and their support of their working-class husbands.

Content Guidance

Social inequality and gender

Evidence relating to gender inequalities

Workplace inequalities for females

The UK labour market can be seen as **horizontally segregated**, meaning that different sectors of employment are dominated by either male or female workers. The Women and Work Commission found that women are disproportionately clustered in specific occupational sectors, dubbed the '5 Cs': cleaning, caring, catering, cashiering (retail) and clerical (administration). For example, women make up about 79% of the health and social work workforce, whereas in the private sector women are over-concentrated in clerical, administrative, retail and personal services, while men are mainly found in the skilled manual and upper professional sectors (Equal Opportunities Commission 2006). Men are ten times more likely than women to be employed in skilled trades and are also more likely to be managers and senior officials.

Horizontal segregation in terms of gender intersects with age, with older women being negatively impacted. Over half of older women work in just three sectors (public administration, health and education). Additionally, 69% of those working in retail are women and many of these are over 50 years old. Jobs in retail and public administration are both at high risk of being replaced by technology. Retail is also one of the sectors, along with hospitality, which accounts for the most minimum-wage jobs.

The UK labour market is also characterised by **vertical segregation**, meaning that males and females dominate different levels of jobs in terms of status, skill and pay. The evidence suggests that, within occupational groups, women tend to be concentrated at the lower levels. When women do gain access to the upper professional or management sector, the evidence suggests that they encounter a **glass ceiling** — they can see the top jobs but restrictions or discrimination create barriers that prevent women getting into them. In 2016, women made up only 20% of senior judges, 21% of business leaders and 29% of MPs.

The Equal Pay Act was passed in 1970, making it unlawful for male and female employees to be paid differently for the same work. An estimated 28,000 equal pay claims per year are accepted at tribunals in the UK, but it is notoriously difficult to prove that one job is substantively 'equal' to another. Equal pay should be distinguished from the **gender pay gap**. According to government statistics, the average UK gender pay gap was 18.1% in 2018. Women's concentration in part-time jobs, which tend to attract lower pay pro rata, is a significant contributor to this — women make up 45% of the workforce but approximately 40% of women work part time. The Fawcett Society describes this as a 'motherhood penalty'.

However, a gender pay gap exists throughout the labour market. Over the last decade, a male graduate could expect to earn 20% more, on average, than a female graduate, with the gap for non-graduates being even wider, at 23%. Since 2017, employers with 250 or more employees have been required to publish data on the gender pay gap in their company. Airlines such as EasyJet and Virgin have been shown to have wide pay gaps, mostly due to the types of jobs within their companies that are held by females and males — with males dominating the higher paid job of pilot and females

---

Horizontal segregation
The divisions between different sectors of the labour market on gendered lines.

Knowledge check 16
Suggest reasons for continuing horizontal segregation in terms of gender and the labour market.

Vertical segregation
The divisions within job sectors in terms of who occupies more senior or junior roles.

Glass ceiling
The invisible barrier which prevents women from climbing to the top levels within occupations.

Gender pay gap
The difference in median earnings received by male and female employees. This can be calculated based on the overall labour force or, more specifically, in different sectors of companies.

being concentrated in cabin crew and administrative roles — demonstrating vertical segregation. The BBC has been widely criticised since publishing its data over the last few years, since most of the highest-paid journalists and presenters are male, with wide differences in pay, which it has found hard to justify.

It is clear that one of the main criteria for disadvantaging women in the workplace relates to childbearing and childcare. The Equality and Human Rights Commission estimated in 2018 that approximately 54,000 women are being unlawfully dismissed or pushed out of their job due to pregnancy. McIntosh (2012) found in his study of nursing that parenthood comes with a tangible 'career penalty' for women, which does not exist for men, in that motherhood results in the devaluation of women's abilities and denial of opportunities, and thus has a direct effect on career progression. Hartnett (1978) discussed the 'myths' associated with employing and promoting women, which often relate back to stereotypes around women as primarily mothers. Employers assume women are less reliable, committed and ambitious due to assumptions about their priorities, whether or not they have children. Such assumptions are not applied to male workers.

Workplace inequalities for males

Although it is clear from the above evidence that females are the gender more likely to be disadvantaged in the workplace in terms of pay and progression, there are some aspects of the workplace which disadvantage males.

Economic changes, in particular the decline in manufacturing and heavy industries such as steel and coal, have had a significant impact on the employment prospects of working-class and older males in certain parts of the UK. This can be linked to the crisis of masculinity discussed by Mac an Ghaill (1994) and the pressure put on the male breadwinner role and hegemonic masculinity. The shift from manufacturing to service industries has been linked to the **feminisation of labour**. Research by the Equality and Human Rights Commission (2015) reveals that the previous 7 years saw a 40% increase in the suicide rate of men aged between 45 and 49, partly blamed on unemployment and financial problems: 'They have seen their jobs, relationships and identities blown apart, and these challenges are exacerbated when men occupy low socioeconomic positions.'

Research by the Department for Business, Innovation and Skills (2015) highlighted another inequality for males related to their role in the workplace. The research found that 69% of fathers have missed a key event in their child's life, with 24% missing their child's first steps and one in five missing their first words. In comparison, just 11% of mothers missed their child's first steps or first words.

The Shared Parental Leave Regulations 2014 allow eligible parents to combine work with family life. Parents can share up to 50 weeks of leave and up to 37 weeks of pay and choose to take the leave or pay flexibly. This has the potential to benefit not only women but also men on the basis of the evidence discussed above. However, in 2018, of the 285,000 couples who were eligible for shared parental leave, only 2% took advantage of the scheme, suggesting that attitudes and inequalities relating to childcare remain entrenched in UK society.

Feminisation of labour The substantial increase in the proportions of women in paid employment since around the 1970s, often linked to the shift in the economy from manufacturing to more service-based industries.

Exam tip

A 20-mark question could focus on female or male disadvantage, or could just refer to gender. Ensure you have a range of evidence for both genders, including workplace inequality, for each but also bringing in other areas, such as education, crime or media representations.

Content Guidance

Explanations for gender inequality

Functionalist explanations

According to functionalists, each institution in society contributes to overall social stability and order. Durkheim (1893) argued that the division of labour was functional for society, and that individuals should take on specialised roles for maximum efficiency.

Functionalists point out that in pre-industrial society men and women took on different roles based on their natural attributes. Men took on hunting roles with responsibility for bringing food to the family, which often took them away from home. Women were limited by pregnancy, childbirth and nursing, so it was more functional for them to take on the farming and gathering roles near the home as well as domestic and childcare roles.

In contemporary society, Talcott Parsons (1956) argues that the nuclear family structure, with a clear-cut sexual division of labour, in which women take on the expressive role and men take on the instrumental role, remains the most efficient way to divide labour. By the expressive role, Parsons means the role of providing care and security to children and offering them emotional support. The instrumental role, in contrast, relates to being the breadwinner in the family and having more concern for the external relationship between the family and other social institutions. Murdock (1949) supports this view, concluding from his cross-cultural comparison of over two hundred societies, that this sexual division of labour, within the nuclear family structure, is universal, since it is the most practical way of organising family responsibilities.

The inequalities experienced by women in the workplace can be further explained using the concept of **human capital**, which can be linked to functionalist ideas of meritocracy. Men are likely to build up more human capital, being more work oriented and career driven, with fewer career breaks and a greater amount of ambition. On the other hand, women are more likely to prioritise their role as a mother over their career. This makes male employees more desirable to employers, and can thus explain pay differences and vertical segregation.

Human capital
The amount of experience, knowledge, personality attributes and skills that a person has, viewed in terms of their value to an employer.

New Right explanations

The New Right would tend to agree with functionalists that gender roles are based on biologically determined differences, and that men and women should play different roles in society, with men taking on roles in the public sphere of work and politics and women staying in the private domestic sphere.

Echoing Parsons' focus on the nuclear family, writers such as Murray (1984) express concerns that more recent changes in gender roles related to family diversity, such as the increase in lone-parent families, dual-career families and same-sex families, have led to social problems. For example, female headed lone-parent families are a concern to Murray, since he feels that children miss out on the clearly defined roles of the father as breadwinner and disciplinarian and the mother as homemaker.

Concern is also expressed that more women are working and leaving their children with no parental bond — which is supported by some psychological theories relating to maternal deprivation, such as Bowlby (1953).

Some writers from the New Right criticise feminism and the increase in females entering the labour market, arguing that this has a detrimental effect not only on children and male partners, but on women themselves. For example, Schlafly (2003) argues that women should see marriage and motherhood as their most important roles and accomplishments. She challenges moves towards equality in the USA, arguing instead that males' and females' differences should be celebrated and that women's main purpose, as mothers, is much more fulfilling for women. Men should earn more, so they can provide for their wives and children, allowing the woman to stay at home and concentrate on childrearing. Schlafly asserts: 'We certainly don't want a society in which the average wage paid to all women equals [that of] men, because that society would have eliminated the role of motherhood'. The small numbers of women in high level roles is evidence of their different priorities and choices, according to Schlafly, rather than of discrimination. Such ideas, relating to women's choices, are echoed by Catherine Hakim (see below).

Evaluation of functionalist and New Right explanations

Both functionalist and New Right approaches to gender inequality have been challenged, particularly by feminists.

For example, Olsen and Walby (2004) challenge the assertions made by both functionalists and the New Right. They argue that women have a disadvantage in acquiring human capital (due to maternity arrangements, employers' assumptions, societal expectations and so on), so to use their lack of human capital to explain their lower pay and status is a circular argument — the main reason for both is the patriarchal system. Ginn et al. (1996) also point out that the 'choice' made by women to prioritise family and childcare is not one that males have to make — they can and do enjoy both with few detrimental effects.

Functionalists and the New Right also tend to ignore the negative effects of the traditional gender roles pointed out by many feminist studies, including domestic abuse within families (e.g. Stanko 2000), sexual harassment and sexism (e.g. Bates 2014) and depression relating to the housewife role (e.g. Oakley 1974).

These theories also overlook the increasing numbers of people who choose to adopt non-traditional gender roles and report positive experiences. Other cultures which have different gender roles, including tribes such as the Chambri, but also Scandinavian countries where parental leave is more commonly shared, can also challenge the 'universal' claim regarding the functionality of traditional gender roles. They are similarly accused of describing a 'golden age' of nuclear families which never really existed — lone parenting, cohabitation and women working have always happened, whether through choice or necessity.

Marxist explanations

Although Marx did not really address gender inequalities, Engels, his colleague, did consider how the control of women in capitalist societies was related to private property ownership and inheritance. In a system which promotes the accumulation of private wealth, it becomes important to ensure paternity in order for bourgeois males to pass on their wealth to their male offspring. For males, in the time before paternity testing was available, the only way to ensure paternity was to have complete control over one's wife. Engels (1972) argued that this accounted for the historical control of

> **Knowledge check 17**
>
> How might feminists explain the arguably self-demeaning views of female writers such as Schlafly and Hakim, and other women who agree with them, that women should embrace motherhood and the housewife role above any kind of career?

Content Guidance

women and their lack of rights and freedom. In contrast, males themselves suffered no such restrictions, being free to have affairs, often with servants, or to take 'a mistress', since this did not interfere with their legitimate heirs.

Weberian explanations

To develop a range of ideas on Weberian explanations for gender inequalities, Weber's concepts of class, status and party can be applied.

By class Weber was referring to market position, which relates to the marketable skills and qualifications an individual has. In terms of gender, it is evident that women have a lower market position than males. This could be linked to various factors such as the glass ceiling, vertical segregation, the gender pay gap or the impact of maternity leave.

Weber saw gender as an aspect of status, recognising that women are perceived in patriarchal societies as having a lower social standing, and consequently fewer rights, by virtue of their gender. This can be seen through evidence of horizontal segregation — the sectors which most involve female workers, such as education and health and social care, also have a lower status in society, perhaps being seen as just an extension of women's domestic role. Feminist ideas on intersectionality (see below) extend these ideas, by showing how various aspects of women's status, including ethnicity, social class, age and sexuality, all intersect to create a hierarchy.

Weber's third source of power was party. For women, lack of social and business connections through the **old boy network** may lead to their exclusion from certain industries and opportunities. Women may also lose their connections and thus their social capital when they take a career break due to having children, and find themselves sidelined on their return to work. This lack of connections has led to various women's networks being formed, which aim to connect women with other women who are in the same industry or experiencing the same barriers. Examples include the Women in Business Network and the Women's Chapter.

The Weberian dual labour market theory of Barron and Norris argues that the economy is divided into two sectors: the high-status primary sector made up of secure, well-paid jobs is dominated by white men, while the low-status secondary sector made up of low-paid, unskilled, part-time, insecure and zero-hour contract jobs is dominated by women.

Barron and Norris argue that women are less likely to gain the status of primary sector employment because employers often subscribe to stereotypical beliefs about the unsuitability of women workers. They may believe that women's careers are likely to be interrupted by pregnancy and childcare, and consequently may be less willing to train or promote them, or may assume that they will not want to work longer hours, for example. Hartnett (1978) discusses some of the 'myths' held by employers, including the idea that workers do not want a female boss, that women are less dependable, that women will not be the main breadwinners of the family and that women will stop work when they have children.

Barron and Norris also point out that the legal and political framework protecting women from such prejudice and discrimination is weak. Relatively few employers have been prosecuted by the Equality and Human Rights Commission or found guilty of gender bias by employment tribunals. For example, in 2010–11, in employment tribunals only 37% of claims against employers for sexual discrimination were successful.

> **Exam tip**
> If asked about Marxist views on gender inequality, include Marxist feminist explanations for gender inequality.

Old boy network
The term relates to upper-class males who attended certain public schools such as Harrow and Eton, and are thus 'old boys' of these institutions. It is sometimes used more widely now to indicate the privileged connections which middle- and upper-class white males may benefit from, which exclude others.

> **Exam tip**
> For any question relating to Weberian explanations, it is a good strategy to develop ideas on class, status and party separately to gain range, supporting each with examples and evidence. The dual labour market theory is also useful to apply to all aspects of inequality.

Section B Understanding social inequalities

Evaluation of Weberian explanations

Bradley (1989) criticises dual labour market theory because it fails to explain inequalities within the same sector. For example, teaching is not a secondary labour market, yet women are less likely than men to gain high-status jobs in this profession.

Feminists would also challenge the view that gender is just an aspect of status, seeing it as a significant source of inequality in its own right, in a patriarchal society.

Feminist explanations

There are a number of feminist theories which aim to explain gendered forms of stratification, including liberal feminism, Marxist feminism and radical feminism.

Liberal feminism

Liberal feminists argue that society is stratified by gender in the sense that men generally dominate the top jobs in societies such as the UK while women generally occupy subordinate positions. Liberal feminists therefore focus on stratification as a patriarchal or male-dominated system.

Liberal feminists argue that patriarchal stratification is mainly the result of gender role socialisation and ideology. Liberal feminists such as Oakley (1981) argue that boys and girls are socialised into socially constructed gender roles. This means that societies such as the UK have clear ideas about what constitutes socially acceptable masculine and feminine types of behaviour. Children are taught this behaviour from a young age by their parents as part of the primary socialisation process. Moreover, these gender roles are reinforced by the peer group, the education system, mass media representations and even religion. Gender role socialisation therefore reproduces a sexual stratification system in which masculinity is seen as dominant and femininity as subordinate.

Gender role socialisation is supported by a dominant patriarchal ideology, which also clearly prescribes particular types of masculine and feminine behaviour that aims to reinforce patriarchal stratification. Oakley argues that the main reason for the subordination of women in the labour market is the dominance of the mother–housewife role. She notes the existence of powerful ideological ideas which serve primarily to ensure men's dominance of the labour market. For example, the ideology that children deprived of their mother's presence may grow up to be psychologically damaged functions to keep women in the home after having children rather than returning to work to compete with men.

Betty Friedan (1963) wrote *The Feminine Mystique* and is often seen as one of the first liberal feminists, paving the way for the second wave of feminism. Through interviews with American housewives, Friedan discovered that many of them suffer from a pervasive and unexplained sense of dissatisfaction, which she dubbed 'the problem that has no name'. This was the underlying dissatisfaction felt by housewives across America that something was missing in their lives. She argues that women were socially pressured into becoming homemakers by the 'feminine mystique': an idealised image of domestic femininity that arose in the 1950s after the Second World War and women's return to domestic life. This feminine mystique was reinforced through education, popular media and the growing consumer culture, through which advertisers sold shiny new kitchen appliances to unhappy housewives. Friedan

> **Exam tip**
>
> In an essay on feminist explanations for gender inequality, ensure you distinguish between the different strands of feminism rather than describing feminists as one group.

Content Guidance

concludes that both genders are subject to the 'mystique' of patriarchy, since they are socialised to see themselves in a certain way, and see it as inevitable.

In the 1990s, liberal feminists suggested that gender stratification was becoming less of a problem. Sue Sharpe's 1994 work on the attitudes of teenage girls suggested that education and careers were a priority for young women, with females recently enjoying great educational success. Other liberal feminists have observed that women have made great progress in terms of the acquisition of economic power through careers, improvements in equal opportunities legislation, political power through greater representation in government, and social power through contraception and divorce. They believe, then, that patriarchal ideology is in decline.

Marxist feminism

See the feminist explanations for class inequality for additional ideas on Marxist feminism, including more on the ideas of Benston, Beechey and Ansley.

Marxist feminists suggest that gender stratification combines with class stratification. Marxist feminists such as Benston (1972) argue that capitalism exploits both male and female workers, but as women are more likely to have children and work part time, they are more likely to be part of a low-paid and often part-time 'reserve army of labour', hired by the capitalist class when the economy is prospering but laid off when recession sets in. This results in women being generally less skilled and relatively under-unionised compared with male workers. Marxists therefore argue that both horizontal and vertical segregation exist because women constitute a more disposable part of the workforce.

This weak occupational position is supported by a patriarchal ideology constructed by agencies such as the family and media that transmits the idea that women belong in the home rather than the workplace, which gives rise to influential ideas that men rather than women should be the family breadwinners. Moreover, when married women do lose their jobs, patriarchal ideology asserts that they have returned to their 'proper' jobs servicing their children and husbands.

Katrine Marçal (2016), in her book *Who Cooked Adam Smith's Dinner?*, questions the fact that economics has long underestimated the value of women's domestic labour to the economy, focusing solely on the contributions of paid labour to the economy. The view that female unpaid labour, in the form of childcare and housework, is a key form of exploitation has previously been argued by other Marxist feminists. For example, Dalla Costa and James (1972) argued that unpaid caring and housework should be recognised and paid, which raised a debate about the value of domestic labour.

Another Marxist feminist analysis comes from Ansley (1976). She argues that women function to soak up male frustration caused by their exploitation at work, referring to women as 'takers of shit'. This is a variation on Parsons' view of the family as a 'warm bath' which can soak away a male worker's stresses and tensions, but from this feminist view women are performing this role in a way which is beneficial to capitalism.

Sheila Rowbotham (1973) wrote that '[m]en will often admit other women are oppressed, but not you'. By this she meant that men often understand the theory of women's oppression but cannot recognise the role they themselves are playing in this oppression. She argues that capitalism operates in combination with patriarchy to

Knowledge check 18

Give some examples of ways in which a female might soak up the stresses of her male partner and thus benefit capitalism according to Ansley.

oppress women, and that while capitalism remains, there is little hope of overthrowing patriarchy, because one supports the other. Women are denied the same opportunities as men, and are thus used as a cheap source of labour, which also undermines men's bargaining position.

Radical feminism

Radical feminists suggest that gender stratification and inequality are far more important than other forms of stratification and inequality. Delphy (1977), for example, argues that men and women constitute separate classes. These classes are organised around exploitation — men exploit women's labour power, especially in the family. This is done mainly via patriarchal ideology (for example, through ideas such as a woman's place is in the home, a real woman has children, children need their mothers) — and physical power, in the form of violence against women.

Radical feminists see all social institutions as being characterised by patriarchy. However, the family is viewed as the main source of patriarchal power because gender role socialisation plants the idea in children that males are dominant and females are subordinate.

In *Sexual Politics* (1970), Kate Millett argues that politics exists in any 'power-structured relationships, arrangements whereby one group of persons is controlled by another'. So a political relationship may exist between males and females in the workplace, in education, in public life and within the family. These relationships are based on patriarchy, therefore the male will always seek to dominate the female. Like liberal feminists such as Friedan and Oakley, Millett looks at the way we are socialised into these roles through **patriarchal ideology**, not just in terms of behaviour (for example, girls being brought up to see housework and childcare as their role), but also in terms of psychology: temperament, belief, confidence and attitude. Millett looks at how biology (including physical strength, vulnerability due to childbirth and sexuality) lies at the root of patriarchal ideology, and also looks at physical dominance (including harassment, violence and rape) as a final way in which males exert their power over women. Millett concludes that the combination of biology, learned roles, ideology and males' physical dominance means that reform is impossible, and a more radical separatism, starting with sexual liberation from heterosexual relationships, is the only way out for women.

Shulasmith Firestone (1970) was influenced by Marx, but she argues that the 'sexual class system' was the first system of stratification, predating the social class system. She argued that inequalities between men and women arose directly from their biological differences, which disadvantaged women, making them dependent on males. This dependence led to males developing a 'power psychology', where men enjoyed their power over women and wished to extend this to power over other men. Firestone uses this to explain both class and racial inequalities, based on this male desire to have power over others. She writes: 'The sexual class system is the model for all other exploitative systems and thus the tapeworm that must be eliminated first by any true revolution.'

The only way to free women from this oppression is to free them from their biology, according to Firestone. Birth control and technology such as *in vitro* fertilisation (IVF) have helped, but full emancipation for women requires them to be freed from the necessity of childbirth and nuclear family relationships completely.

Patriarchal ideology

This refers to the set of ideas about society based on views about the natural dominance and superiority of men, which are presented as natural and inevitable, and which feminists argue we are all socialised into accepting.

Content Guidance

Evaluation of feminist explanations

Liberal feminism has been criticised by Walby (1990), who argues that although there is evidence that masculinity and femininity are socially constructed, this does not explain why men are usually in positions of dominance. Liberal feminism also implies that women passively accept their gender identities.

The optimism of some liberal feminists is also challenged. Both horizontal and vertical forms of job segregation by gender still exist, as does the gender pay gap. Barron and Norris's dual labour market theory also undermines the liberal feminist assumption that better qualifications and changes in women's ambitions will automatically dismantle gender divisions in employment.

Additionally, in common with the other strands of feminism, liberal feminism has been accused of treating women's experience of patriarchal stratification as a universal experience. Women's experiences may qualitatively differ according to their social class position as well as their ethnic and religious statuses. More recent feminists tend to have embraced the idea of intersectionality, considering the ways in which gender intersects with other sources of discrimination. This is considered further in the ethnicity and age sections.

Marxist feminism has been criticised for failing to convincingly explain why jobs are gendered, that is, why women occupy the housewife role or dominate certain sectors of work. If women are cheaper than men to employ, surely it would be more profitable for the capitalist class to replace the male workforce with a cheaper female workforce. Additionally, the challenges which are applied to Marxism, namely that capitalism is the most successful and widespread economic system, which is strengthening rather than weakening and unlikely to be overthrown, would also apply to Marxist feminism.

Radical feminists are challenged for their extreme views, which might alienate many male and female supporters of equality. Like Marxist feminists, they can be seen as unrealistic in their aims, since patriarchy is so ingrained that a revolutionary change is unlikely, and the more reformist approach of liberal feminists is arguably more achievable.

Catherine Hakim (2006) is critical of all the above feminist positions. She argues that feminist theories of gender stratification are both inaccurate and misleading. Women are not victims of unfair employment practices because women with children make rational choices about their futures — they believe that childcare is just as important as employment. Consequently, the lack of women in top jobs and their domination of part-time work does not reflect employer discrimination, weak laws, gender role socialisation or patriarchal ideology, but rather women's rational choice to be mothers and homemakers.

Another criticism of feminist views on gender inequality is that such views are now outdated. The feminist views discussed mostly originated in the 1960s and 1970s and many of the goals of the original feminists have been achieved. For example, girls are now doing better than boys in education and are more likely to go to university, there are more women in the workforce and in more senior positions than ever, and there is equality legislation enshrining these rights in law. However, today's feminists would challenge this assertion.

> **Exam tip**
>
> The disagreements within feminism, from the different strands of feminism (including black feminism, see below), can be a good source of evaluation.

Section B Understanding social inequalities

Newer feminist views

Banyard (2011) argues in *The Equality Illusion* that despite the strides made by women towards equality, the gender pay gap and issues such as horizontal and vertical segregation remain significant. She also highlights the growing issue of violence and sexual abuse against women, a theme picked up by other current feminists. Faludi (1993) wrote of a 'backlash' against women from men who were seeing their privileged position as under attack from feminism. This trend has also been noted by many more recent feminist writers, recognising the growth in 'lad culture' and the increase in misogyny, both offline and online. Bates (2018), in *Misogynation: The True Scale of Sexism*, develops the themes she has highlighted through her Everyday Sexism project, discussing the continued prevalence of unacceptable sexualised behaviour that has become normalised by society, including catcalling and other seemingly casual harassment, from comments and touching to aggressive and threatening tweets.

> **Knowledge check 19**
>
> In what ways can the everyday sexism and the laddish culture highlighted by some current feminists be seen as a backlash against feminism?

Summary: gender inequality

- There are distinct inequalities in the work experiences and opportunities of men and women, which negatively impact on life chances. For women, these include issues of horizontal and vertical segregation, and for men they relate to a 'crisis of masculinity' related to the loss of the breadwinner role for some men.
- Functionalist and New Right sociologists tend to focus on the biological differences between males and females to explain their concentration in different jobs and roles.
- Weberian explanations would focus on the inferior market position and status of females as a reason for their lack of power and access to equality.
- Marxists and Marxist feminists consider the way in which capitalism may benefit from gender inequalities endemic in a patriarchal society, whereas liberal feminists are more optimistic and, while blaming patriarchal ideology behind the socialisation of males and females into their assigned gender roles, do argue that things are slowly changing.
- Radical feminists are less optimistic and argue that the inequalities faced by females are rooted in male power and that biology is used to justify women's oppression. Newer feminists tend to support such views by showing that, where male power and dominance have been challenged by feminism, misogyny has increased.

Social inequality and ethnicity

Evidence relating to ethnic inequalities

Workplace

There are clear patterns related to ethnicity in terms of the labour market. Men from certain minority ethnic groups including Pakistani, Bangladeshi and African Caribbean, are over-represented in the low-skilled, low-paid and insecure service sector, particularly in the restaurant and retail industries. In contrast, few people from these ethnic backgrounds are engaged in white-collar, professional or managerial

Content Guidance

work. However, people from Indian and Chinese backgrounds are more likely than other ethnic groups to be found in middle-class non-manual occupations such as accountancy, law and medicine. For example, approximately 1 in 20 working Indian men in the UK is a medical practitioner — almost ten times the national average.

In 2017, in every region in England, Wales and Scotland, unemployment rates were higher for people from minority ethnic groups (other than white minorities) compared with white people. The unemployment rate for those from white ethnic backgrounds was 4%, whereas the rate for those from Pakistani and Bangladeshi backgrounds was 10% and from black backgrounds was 9%.

In 2009, researchers from the National Centre for Social Research sent out nearly 3,000 job applications under false identities using the surnames of Mahmood, Namagembe and Taylor. Each application had a similar level of work experience, a British education, a good set of qualifications and excellent work histories. The researchers found that the Taylor identity sent out on average nine applications before receiving an invitation for an interview, while the Mahmood and Namagembe identities had to send out an average of 16 applications before they received a positive response.

Such research supports claims that an **ethnic penalty** exists in the labour market. Heath and Cheung (2006) found evidence of an ethnic penalty in the labour market in their research, concluding that Pakistani, Bangladeshi, Black Caribbean and Black African men continue to experience higher unemployment rates, greater concentrations in routine and semi-routine work and lower hourly earnings than members of the comparison group of British and other white groups. They contend that these differentials cannot be explained by the age, education or foreign birth of those from minority ethnic groups, since they apply even for the second generation, born and educated in Britain.

Ashong-Lamptey (2014) considers reasons for the lack of people from minority ethnic backgrounds in professional occupations such as law and accountancy. These reasons include the culture and identity of such professions, which may lead to self-selection or exclusion, as some feel they are not for 'people like them'. The professions themselves also contribute to this, by choosing candidates from Russell Group universities, for example, which suffer from an under-representation of students from minority ethnic backgrounds, and also by not choosing those who deviate from their corporate image.

In his study of recruitment practices, Jenkins (1986) investigated how potential job applicants were assessed. He found that the two main criteria used were 'suitability' and 'acceptability'. Suitability related to whether candidates had the relevant skills and qualifications for the job, assessed through the application form and CV. Acceptability related to more qualitative assessments made at interview about a candidate's 'manner', 'appearance' and 'attitude'. Candidates from minority ethnic backgrounds who were judged 'suitable' were often unsuccessful in their applications based on 'acceptability'. Jenkins discovered through his interviews with human resources managers that such judgements were related to considerations of who would 'fit in' with the company and current staff, often based on managers' gut feelings and racial stereotypes.

> **Exam tip**
>
> Avoid making generalised claims about 'ethnic minorities'. It is important to recognise that there are differences between ethnic groups, and that some minority ethnic groups are achieving more highly than the white majority.

> **Ethnic penalty**
>
> A penalty based purely on ethnicity, when all other factors (such as qualifications and experience and also age, class and gender) are taken into account.

> **Exam tip**
>
> Aim to ensure your language is inclusive as well as accurate. Use terms such as 'minority ethnic employees' or 'those from BAME (black, Asian and minority ethnic) backgrounds'. Everyone has an ethnicity, including the majority, so avoid referring to 'ethnics'!

Racial discrimination within the workplace also remains an issue. The business network Employers in the Community, in 2018, found that one in three employees from minority ethnic backgrounds had experienced racial harassment or bullying from managers in the previous 2 years, and that there was an increase in those who had witnessed or experienced racial harassment or bullying from customers or service users — up to 19% from 16% in the previous year.

Explanations for ethnic inequality

Theoretical approaches to explaining ethnic inequality can be broadly divided into cultural explanations and structural explanations.

Cultural explanations suggest that ethnic disadvantage can be explained in terms of the cultural origins and values of minority ethnic people. The relevance of culture may include issues of language, and also norms and values relating to cultural traditions, which may influence choices surrounding education, career paths and so on. Cultural explanations would include functionalism and the New Right.

Structural explanations contend that ethnic disadvantage is caused by the organisation and structure of capitalist society — in particular, the focus on competition and market principles. Minority ethnic groups tend to have lower levels of status and so they will lose out in the struggle for money, jobs and power. From this perspective, the ruling class has a vested interest in perpetuating racism for two main reasons. First, if minority ethnic workers are seen as 'inferior', they will be easier to exploit as a source of cheap labour, and, second, creating a sense of competition between workers of different ethnicities will lead to a divided working class, in which minority ethnic groups become scapegoats for issues such as low pay and unemployment, distracting attention from structural class inequalities and making all workers easier to control. Marxism is the main structural explanation, but Weberians and feminists would also focus on the structure of society as the basis of ethnic inequality.

Functionalist explanations

Durkheim's ideas on value consensus, norms, values and culture can be used to explain inequalities of outcome for people from minority ethnic groups. The cultural differences of immigrant communities, coupled with their relatively low level of skills, can explain why they have experienced exclusion from certain sectors of the job market, for example. Functionalists are optimistic that in a meritocratic society ethnic inequalities would decline as immigrants adopted the norms and values of mainstream society.

Patterson's host immigrant model (1965) develops Durkheim's ideas, suggesting that the value consensus among the majority 'hosts' of a country will be challenged by the arrival of immigrants with different norms and values. This results in a culture clash, and inevitably leads to racism and discrimination, as the hosts feel threatened by the alien culture of the immigrants. Patterson suggests that such clashes are based on understandable fears and anxieties on the part of the host community. Inequalities and discrimination experienced by those from minority ethnic groups are thus based on the host culture's fear of the cultural difference of the immigrant 'strangers' and the threat this poses to social order, and their resentment of having to compete with

> **Knowledge check 20**
> How could you use some of this evidence to apply the concepts of vertical segregation and the glass ceiling to ethnicity and the workplace?

immigrants for scarce resources such as jobs and housing. The key cause of this fear and resentment relates to a lack of **assimilation** to the host culture. Patterson was optimistic that if immigrants move towards full cultural assimilation by shedding their 'old' values and taking on the values of the host society, discrimination and inequalities would disappear.

Talcott Parsons' ideas on meritocracy can also be applied to explain ethnic inequalities. He would point to the evidence that some minority ethnic groups, such as those of Indian and Chinese origin, do better in education and also are more likely to enter professional occupations than any other ethnic groups. This suggests that racism or any kind of ethnic discrimination is not present within the education system or labour market, and instead they are working meritocratically. Those who get the best qualifications, due to hard work and talent, will then go on to secure the best jobs. This could be supported with evidence of a Chinese focus on academic success found by Francis and Archer (2005), among others. The emphasis put on educational excellence and the hard work encouraged within that ethnic group explains their excellent outcomes, suggesting that the blame for any negative outcomes experienced by those from other ethnic groups lies within their own cultural attitudes rather than in any lack of opportunities or racial discrimination.

New Right explanations

The New Right would tend to support Parsons' ideas on meritocracy. Murray and Herrnstein's controversial study, *The Bell Curve* (1994), identified a link between ethnicity and intelligence quotient (IQ), which they used to explain lower achievements and outcomes for African Americans in the USA. This evidence has been widely challenged, not least because IQ tests themselves are shown to be culturally biased and thus unreliable.

Murray also links his ideas on cultural deprivation and the underclass to ethnicity. His 'tripod' of indicators of an underclass comprises 'illegitimacy, violent crime, and drop-out from the labour force' (1989). By illegitimacy, he was particularly referring to unmarried young women having children and relying on the state to support them, with the biological fathers not taking responsibility for the consequences of their actions. His argument is that children brought up in such families are inadequately socialised into a dependency culture, lacking a strong work ethic or any positive role models, which can then explain their negative outcomes in education and employment. The link to ethnicity was made by Murray in the claim that people from certain ethnic groups, in particular African Americans in the USA, are more likely to have children without being married, and women from these ethnic backgrounds were more likely to be left to raise these children alone. Such a link has also been made to African Caribbeans in the UK, although this has been challenged, and the statistical basis is shaky. Some support for this premise has come from Sewell (1997), who found that 57% of African Caribbean families with dependent children were headed by lone parents, compared with 25% of white families.

Evaluation of cultural explanations (relevant for both functionalist and New Right arguments)

Some specific evaluation of Patterson's host immigrant model includes the view that it cannot be assumed that all minority ethnic groups can or should assimilate into 'British culture'. Some would argue that Britain is a multicultural society in which different ethnic cultures coexist side by side and that this diversity should be

Assimilation Adopting the norms and values of the host culture in order to fully integrate and fit in.

Exam tip

It is a good idea to combine explanations if you feel you do not have enough range for a 40-mark essay. Functionalists and the New Right can be used to support and extend each other, and the same is sometimes true of Marxist and Weberian ideas.

celebrated, while others would question whether there is a clear 'British culture' to assimilate to, given the diversity within British culture. This argument is extended by those who point out that assimilation is only possible if the hosts allow it: many in the UK show hostility towards immigrants, advocating segregation rather than integration, for example in terms of housing, which prevents assimilation.

Marxists would criticise Patterson for ignoring the role that capitalism plays and how the division of people by race helps to maintain the capitalist structure. This means that assimilation is impossible to achieve under capitalism.

Cultural explanations are often accused of 'blaming the victim' for their own discriminatory treatment. A focus on the differences in culture can lead to the inflexible attitude that 'they' are to blame for having different norms and values. This has the effect of removing blame from structural factors such as racism in the workplace or the lack of suitable employment opportunities in the locality.

Gilroy (1990) challenges cultural explanations for what he calls the 'fallacy of ethnic absolutism'. This is the assumption that ethnic cultures are 'fixed' and 'final'. Gilroy contends that cultures are dynamic and diverse, not static or homogeneous. They are also continually evolving and are affected by social context and the situation that members of the culture find themselves in. Instead of blaming the culture of a particular ethnic group for the negative outcomes they experience, such as racism and exclusion, it needs to be recognised that those negative experiences have an effect on the evolution of the culture and the way its members behave. Thus Gilroy argues that cultural explanations are blaming the victims of racial disadvantage for their situation, rather than recognising that this disadvantage is what causes the culture to adapt.

Marxist explanations

From a Marxist perspective, capitalism creates a conflict between the privileged ruling class and the oppressed working class. Most members of minority ethnic groups are also members of the working class and it is this, rather than their ethnicity or culture, which explains their disadvantaged position.

Cox (1970) argues that 'racism' is socially constructed, and was created and encouraged to benefit capitalism and the exploitation of labour. The success of early capitalism was linked to colonialism and the spread of European empires. As European nations conquered other areas of the world, they exploited the workforce in those colonies and they justified their actions through racism, by claiming that white Europeans were superior to other races. This view made the immorality of slavery easier for the white Christian plantation owners and early capitalists to justify.

In a Marxist study of immigrant workers in Britain, Castles and Kosack (1973) found that most immigrants were concentrated in low-skilled and low-paid manual jobs that were mainly carried out in poor working conditions, or were unemployed. Castles and Kosack claimed that in Britain this treatment of immigrants came from the need for a reserve army of labour. It was necessary to have a surplus of labour power in order to keep wage costs down, since the greater the overall supply of labour power, the weaker the bargaining position of existing workers became. Capitalist economies are inherently unstable. They undergo periods of boom and slump, and a reserve army of labour needs to be available to be hired and fired as the fluctuating fortunes of

Knowledge check 21

Explain why assimilation is a two-way process.

Content Guidance

the economy dictate. After the Second World War, as Britain embarked on a massive rebuilding and restructuring programme, immigrants from former colonies were actively brought into the country to provide a necessary cheap pool of workers who could be profitably exploited.

The arrival of immigrants led to the working class being divided into two groups, with the white population becoming the top layer of the working class and the immigrant workers becoming a distinctive grouping at the bottom. Castles and Kosack argue this 'divide and rule' tactic was beneficial to the ruling class as it suppressed the overall wage levels of the working class, and immigrants could be scapegoated (blamed) for problems such as unemployment and housing shortages, thus allowing the bourgeoisie to divert the white working class's attention from the real cause of inequalities. Furthermore, this situation meant that the working class became too divided to unite and overthrow the capitalist system.

Like Cox, neo-Marxist Miles (1989) argues that racism was originally used to justify the exploitation of non-Europeans in various parts of the world. However, Miles goes on to argue that, by the end of colonialism, the type of racism that saw different types of biological grouping as superior or inferior to others was replaced with nationalism, in which individuals saw their nation as superior to other nations. Miles is also influenced by Weberian theory as he argues that the concept of status should be used alongside the concept of class to explain racism and racial inequality. Miles argues that the class position of those from minority ethnic groups is complicated by their racist and exclusionary treatment by much of the white population, which may in turn lead some from the minority ethnic group to resist and set themselves apart from the white majority by stressing and celebrating their own cultural uniqueness; for example, young African Caribbeans may celebrate their black identity through rap music (this can link to Gilroy's concept of the 'Black Atlantic identity'), while Asians may stress the importance of family ties and community through where they choose to live and who they choose to marry.

Miles argues that as a result of these two processes, the working class divides into **racialised class fractions**, preventing any sense of class affinity between people from different ethnic groups within the working class. This may also occur within the middle class — as increasing numbers of people from minority ethnic groups enter middle-class professions, many white middle-class professionals may not accept them as equal in status. This means that even when those from minority ethnic groups do not experience social class inequality, they are not immune to experiencing status inequality.

Evaluation of Marxist explanations

Critics of Cox would argue that it is too simplistic to suggest that racism is only found in capitalist societies. Although it may benefit capitalism in some ways, some of the negative implications of racism could damage capitalist societies. Additionally, racism arguably existed in other social systems predating capitalism, and does exist in present-day non-capitalist societies.

Furthermore, critics challenge Marxism as an 'economic reductionist' theory. This means that it tends to reduce all inequalities to issues of social class and the structure

Racialised class fractions Divisions within a social class along racial or ethnic lines, preventing a cohesive class identity from forming.

Knowledge check 22

Identify three ways in which racism could be seen to benefit capitalism.

Exam tip

Some neo-Marxist ideas, like those of Miles, link to Weberian ones, so you could use them together in an essay, but make clear why you are making the link between them.

of the economy. While racial and class conflicts are connected, race and racism are important sources of inequality in their own right.

Although Marxists like Castles and Kosack describe the exploitation of those from minority ethnic groups as part of the class struggle, critics would argue that many minority ethic people are not disadvantaged. For example, recent statistics suggest that many of those in the wealthiest proportion of the UK are from such backgrounds, including the Hinduja brothers, who are the UK's wealthiest men.

Weberian explanations

Members of minority ethnic groups are distributed across all social classes. Weber's ideas on the intersection between class (market position), status (social standing in society) and party (membership/access to certain groups) recognise the importance in the difference *between* classes but also *within* classes, based on other, non-economic factors, including ethnicity.

Class status and party as applied to ethnicity

When considering Weber's ideas on class, by which he meant market position, factors such as knowledge, qualifications, experience, skills and desirability to employers are important. Members of certain ethnic groups in the UK have a superior market and work situation based on their educational outcomes, social background and contacts, for example. Class can intersect with status, however, since, as evidenced above, even those with equivalent qualifications may find their ethnicity disadvantages them in the labour market.

Weberians consider ethnicity as an aspect of status. An ethnic group can be seen as a status group, sharing a similar degree of prestige or respect. Minority ethnic groups in Britain may have lower status due to the influence of racist ideologies. Status groups can be competitive and aim to achieve social closure, which means that they try to monopolise privilege and exclude other groups from their positions of privilege. In terms of ethnicity, this could mean that status and power are in the hands of those from the majority ethnic group, thereby making it difficult for minority ethnic groups to compete equally for jobs, housing and so on. For example, Parkin (1968) argued that minority ethnic groups are **negatively privileged status groups**. Privileged status groups (the white majority) can operate social closure, preventing minority groups from reaching positions of authority.

Status can also divide a class group or even cut across class differences. For instance, minority ethnic manual workers may have a lower status than white manual workers, and minority ethnic middle-class professionals may experience status inequality in the form of prejudicial attitudes held by members of both the white middle class and the white working class. Those from minority ethnic groups, therefore, not only suffer from social class inequality, they also suffer from status inequality — ideas which are developed by Miles (see above).

In terms of party, by which Weber meant membership of a group or organisation which can bring power, those from minority ethnic groups may find themselves socially excluded from 'the Establishment' of British society. For example, fewer students from certain minority ethnic backgrounds receive offers from Oxbridge and Russell Group universities or attend the top public schools. Membership of certain exclusive associations and clubs (such as 'gentlemen's clubs', golf clubs or the freemasons) often

Negatively privileged status groups Those who are looked down on in society by others who seek to maintain their privileged status, and who are consequently denied full access to opportunities others may enjoy.

comes through nomination from existing members, making it difficult for those from different communities to access. This can be linked to the idea of the old boy network and also Bourdieu's concept of **social capital**.

Another Weberian-influenced view which can be applied to explain ethnic inequality is Barron and Norris's dual labour market theory. They suggest that the labour market can be divided into the primary sector — comprising permanent, well-paid and high-status careers — and the secondary sector — made up of part-time or temporary low-status jobs. Those from certain minority ethnic backgrounds are more likely to find themselves in the secondary labour market. This may be due to disadvantages experienced in education, leading to fewer qualifications, but may also be a result of the weak legal framework protecting their rights, as well as discrimination by employers (often based on 'myths' relating to stereotypical assumptions about cultural differences).

Weberians Rex and Tomlinson (1979) argue that minority ethnic experience of both class and status inequality has led to a poverty-stricken black underclass, isolated from the white working class and experiencing disadvantage with regard to the labour market, housing and education. These disadvantages were worsened by the hostility directed at them by white society. This black underclass felt socially excluded from the standard of living that most other members of society took for granted, and victimised by overzealous policing, which they experienced as harassment. These feelings had the potential to occasionally erupt in the form of inner-city riots.

Evaluation of Weberian explanations

The Weberian approach is more flexible than the Marxist model, seeming better able to deal with the scattered class positions and economic progress of different ethnic groups. Marxists would, however, accuse Weberians of failing to recognise the basic problem — the exploitative nature of capitalism, from which all other inequalities of status will flow. Critics may also argue that Weberian theory still does not provide any way to distinguish between the relative importance of the different types of inequality.

Weberians who emphasise the low status of those from minority ethnic groups, such as Parkin, and Rex and Tomlinson, have been criticised for overemphasising minority ethnic groups as passive victims of racism. Owen and Green (1992) point out that the position of minority ethnic groups is changing and some groups, particularly Chinese and Indian people, are outperforming their counterparts from other ethnicities at school and are faring well in the labour market too. New Right commentators would blame the culture of some minority ethnic groups for the poverty and unemployment that their members experience.

Feminist explanations

Feminists focus on explaining gender inequalities, but the main strands of feminism — liberal, radical and Marxist — have been criticised for generalising about women and not recognising the differences in the experiences and inequalities which women face in terms of their social class, age, sexuality and ethnicity. The issue of inequalities experienced by women of colour has most notably been raised by postcolonial and black feminism, which are closely affiliated.

> **Social capital** This is a concept used by Bourdieu to describe the amount and quality of the social contacts an individual may have, which can bring them advantages and power.

Section B Understanding social inequalities

Postcolonial theory was developed by those in or from previously colonised parts of the world as a resistance against the narrative of the Western colonial powers and their 'civilising' agenda, and in recognition of the enduring influence and impact of this agenda. Postcolonial feminism originated in the 1980s, to highlight the experience of women of colour in, or originating from, the former colonies (including, for example, parts of Africa, the Caribbean and Asia). For example, Peterson and Rutherford (1986) argue that feminist analyses of gender inequality fail to consider 'double colonisation'. BAME women are doubly oppressed by patriarchy but also by ethnocentrism of white middle-class feminism that ignores or neglects the unique problems faced by BAME women.

One of the most influential black feminists is bell hooks (she uses lowercase letters to distinguish her name from that of her grandmother). In *Ain't I a Woman?* (1981), hooks articulates her frustration with the failure of the black liberation movement and the women's liberation movement to include the concerns of black women, arguing that race and sex are intertwined aspects of identity and cannot be understood apart from each other. The title comes from a famous speech made in 1851 by the black female slave and campaigner Sojourner Truth, which illustrates the differences in the way that white women and black women have traditionally been seen by men, through describing her experience as a black slave. White women were seen as vulnerable, weak, inferior and in need of protection, stereotypes which have been the source of much feminist challenge, but hooks argues that the problem for black women historically has been very different. During slavery, due to being both black and female, black female slaves experienced the brunt of misogyny combined with racism. Since hatred of sexuality was embedded in American culture, the female became both a source of lust and a threat to male morale. Therefore, black women were subjected to widespread sexual and physical abuse which was widely ignored by both white and black communities.

In more recent times, hooks argues that black women have been marginalised in civil rights campaigns: 'When black people are talked about the focus tends to be on black men; and when women are talked about the focus tends to be on white women.' She claims that black nationalism seeks to recreate racist patriarchy, with black men at the top of the social hierarchy. Her later works embraced a wider intersectionality, which is further discussed in the age inequality section. However, she clearly believes that racist imperialism — along Marxist lines — lies at the heart of ethnic inequality, which together with patriarchy has a particularly devastating effect on women of colour.

Other black feminists also challenge the ethnocentric agenda of mainstream feminism, for neglecting the differences in the inequalities and discrimination experienced by women of colour in particular, and pursuing an equality agenda which focuses on white middle-class priorities. For example, Mirza (1997) claims that women of colour can challenge the distorted assumptions of a variety of dominant groups, not just males, by drawing on their own experiences.

Another influential American black feminist is Patricia Hill Collins. In 1990 she discussed the history of black women working in domestic roles in the homes of

Knowledge check 23

What is meant by 'intersectionality'?

Content Guidance

the white wealthy classes in the USA, and points out that although black women have moved on from such jobs in today's America, they are still concentrated in the lowest-paid work. Another area of oppression affecting black women considered by Collins (2006) is the portrayal of young black women in overtly sexualised ways — for example, in the hip-hop genre. Because such portrayals are perpetuated by black males, they are often overlooked as a key example of racism.

Evaluation of feminist explanations

By focusing on the intersection between ethnicity and gender, postcolonial and black feminists have been accused of undermining the importance of both racism and patriarchy as separate oppressive structures. For example, black feminists have been accused of creating divisions within feminism rather than helping women to unite against patriarchy. A similar charge could be made in relation to racism — by challenging the sexism of black males, they may be undermining the collective fight against racism.

> **Exam tip**
>
> The ideas of black feminists can be used to evaluate other feminist explanations for gender inequality as well as to explain ethnic inequality.

> **Summary: ethnic inequality**
>
> - Evidence suggests that people from certain minority ethnic groups experience significant barriers, which result in their under-representation in well-paid professional and skilled manual jobs and increase their potential to be unemployed.
> - Cultural explanations of ethnic inequality, which include functionalism and the New Right, tend to focus on the norms and values of certain ethnic groups, and their failure to assimilate or to have the appropriate work ethic. Such views can be controversial and seen as 'blaming the victim'.
> - Marxists focus their explanations for ethnic inequality on the needs of capitalism, considering how racism can be used to justify exploitation and how minority ethnic groups have been used as a reserve army of labour.
> - From a Weberian perspective, ethnicity is most understood as an aspect of status, and there is a recognition that those from minority ethnic groups lack status in UK society, which can explain discriminatory practices.
> - Black feminists highlight the different treatment experienced by black women, showing that ethnicity and gender intersect as sources of inequality and neither can be understood in isolation.

Social inequality and age

Evidence relating to age inequalities

Age intersects with other structural influences such as class, gender and ethnicity and results in inequalities experienced by both elderly and young people.

Workplace inequalities for older people

In industrial societies, older people are seen as lacking the ability to contribute meaningfully and are often excluded from full involvement in society. This social exclusion has two major effects.

Many older people are forced to work past retirement age because they did not earn enough over their lifetime to put away savings or they worked for employers who did not run private pension schemes. Older women, in particular, are more likely to be in poverty than older men because they live longer and they generally receive less from earnings-linked private pension funds after taking time out of the labour market to raise children, with the result that they did not contribute as much of their wage to this future benefit. There is also some evidence that older people may fail to claim the state benefits to which they are entitled because they are unaware of them or they are too embarrassed or proud to claim the money. Department for Work and Pensions statistics (2018) suggest that just 60% of eligible poorer people of pension age claim the pension credit to which they are entitled.

There is much evidence to suggest ageism in the workplace, which Gratton (2018) argues begins at 40 for women and 45 for men. Many employees' careers peaked at these ages and they were no longer considered for promotion or training. The government's Women and Equalities Committee supports this, finding in 2018 that over 1 million people over 50 have been pushed out of the workplace.

The recruitment website CV-Library conducted research in 2017 which found that one-third of workers claimed that they had been rejected for a job because of their age, and over half of workers aged over 55 said they had been treated unfavourably because of their age.

Ray et al. (2006) found that employers assume lower competence from older workers, which can lead to exclusion from the workplace and also from more senior positions. However, they argue that in experiments it has been shown that there is no difference in levels of competence, so this assumption is a myth based on ageist stereotypes rather than any actual evidence.

Jenkins' 2008 study of ageism in the hotel industry found evidence of indirect age discrimination in terms of recruitment and selection for employment. For example, recruitment usually took place via the internet, which could link to the generational digital divide in preventing older people from applying. Additionally, hotels tend to use colleges to recruit students for casual work and rely on word of mouth, further excluding older potential employees. Furthermore, in the selection of candidates, Jenkins found that importance was placed on appearance and on replacing people with someone similar, which also indirectly discriminated against older candidates.

Phillipson et al. (2016) found that jobs available to older people are less desirable, citing evidence that firms with poorer progression and training opportunities are more likely to recruit older workers. Lain (2012) found that employees working at age 65–69 who had been recruited since 2000 were disproportionately in 'Lopaq' occupations: low paid, part time and requiring few qualifications. This may be because such jobs are less desirable to the 'prime working age' population.

Workplace inequalities for younger people

Younger workers are often subject to worse pay and conditions than those from any other age groups. This can be linked to their concentration in the secondary labour market and their use as a reserve army of labour: students often take on part-time, temporary and low-paid work and are used to fill in gaps in the labour force, for example at peak times such as Christmas and at times when other workers are less available, such as the summer. Young workers are also much less likely to be members of trade unions, which means they have less power in the workplace. This can be linked to Weber's idea of 'party'.

There is much evidence to suggest that discrimination against younger workers is widespread, which may relate to employers' stereotypical attitudes towards youths. Loretto et al. (2000) support this, finding that younger employees often come across discriminatory practices, including lower wages, poorer working conditions and an attitude of mistrust relating to their skills, competence and commitment. Sweiry and Willitts' 2012 study of age-related prejudice in the UK showed that younger age groups (below 25) were more likely to see age discrimination as more serious than older groups (over 64). The CV-Library website's 2018 research found that over half of under 18s feel they are not taken seriously at work, and three-quarters of 25- to 34-year-olds say they have been discriminated against for being 'too young'.

The law ensures equal pay for equal work, preventing discrimination against an individual worker based on their gender or ethnicity. However, it is legal for employers to pay someone differently based on age, even where they are doing exactly the same job. The legal minimum wage is significantly lower for those under 18, 21 and 25 years of age. For example, using April 2020 figures, the minimum or 'living' wage for those over 25 is £8.72 per hour, but for those between 21 and 24 it is £8.20, 18- to 20-year-olds get at least £6.45, whereas those under 18 get £4.55. Additionally, those doing an apprenticeship, who are more likely to be younger people, will be paid a minimum of £4.15 per hour.

In the first part of 2019, the youth unemployment rate (12.2%) was more than three times higher than the overall unemployment rate (3.8%), though both rates have been steadily falling. There is also evidence that more young people are dependent on their parents for a greater length of time. The increase in the value of property combined with low pay and/or rates of employment means it is virtually impossible for some young people to get on the property ladder. Furthermore, the number of young homeless people has increased.

Health inequalities for older people

The National Health Service (NHS) has been accused of **institutional ageism**. Elderly people may be offered fewer healthcare choices, for example, due to assumptions that they have lower expectations about their health. Additionally, Greengross (1997) argues that there are views on 'a good innings' within the health service — meaning that if people are in later old age they are seen to have had their

Exam tip

If the question is not focused specifically on older people, discuss the impact of ageism on those in the younger age groups as well. Students often forget this. You could also be asked specifically about disadvantages experienced by older or younger people.

Institutional ageism
Ingrained norms and values within an organisation which operate to unfairly discriminate in terms of age.

time — and if a patient is over that age, additional medical interventions will often not be considered or offered to them.

Geriatric medicine has a lower status in the NHS, which could lead to fewer medical professionals specialising in this area. Moreover, lack of resources relating to health and social care arrangements mean many older people are stuck in hospital because there is no one to care for them at home. Hockey and James (1993) found that elderly people are 'infantilised' (treated like children) in institutional care — often patronised and assumed to be senile.

Craig and Mindell considered the health of older people, using data from the Health Survey for England in 2005, based on responses from those over 65. Over half described themselves as being in good or very good health. However, 37% of men and 40% of women had some degree of disability and the numbers increased with age.

Gender and class differences in older people were also noticed in terms of health. For example:

- Older women were more likely than men to have a chronic illness or condition that affected their lives in some way.
- Men were more likely than women to have poor social capital in the sense of friends, family and social networks. Poor health was linked to poor social capital, with those who experienced bad health also being those who saw fewest people and who went out least often.
- Older men were more likely to suffer from heart disease, whereas older women were more likely to experience mobility problems and were more vulnerable to falling.
- Those in the wealthier income brackets ate more fresh fruit and vegetables. Anaemia and vitamin D deficiency caused by lack of adequate diet or lack of sunshine were more common among those in the lower income groups.

A final issue relating to older people and health relates to expectations and issues of identity. Older people often *expect* to experience mental and physical symptoms in later life and consequently fail to mention symptoms to their doctors, even when effective treatments exist (Williams 1990). Bond and Corner (2004) support this, suggesting that 'common-sense' stereotypes lead many older people to accept that ill health is an inevitable part of human ageing. Corner (1999) also found that older people described the 'problems' of old age for society and the 'burden' of the ageing population. They were concerned with becoming a 'burden' and saw later life as one of ill health and dependency. Corner found that the majority of participants in his study were likely to attribute many of the medical conditions for which they were being treated to 'old age'.

Explanations for age inequality

Functionalist and New Right explanations

Parsons (1962) has discussed the differences in the social roles associated with different age groups as vital for the smooth functioning of society. He sees childhood as a key period of primary socialisation within the family, with children as empty vessels being filled with the agreed norms and values of society. The period of youth is the transitional period between childhood and adulthood, seen as a 'bridge' between

Exam tip

Due to the narrowness of material relating to age inequality (and also gender), you could link functionalist and New Right ideas together in an essay to get more range, making it clear that they are based on similar ideas.

these two worlds. Youths start to become independent from their parents, but in complex modern societies this protracted period is essential for individuals to learn the necessary skills and to make mistakes in the relatively safe and risk-free environment, before important responsibilities such as having a job and raising a family arrive. So Parsons sees youth culture as an important 'rite of passage', which individuals must complete. It is thus understandable that during this transitional phase, young people are not given the full rights and responsibilities of adults, including being paid less and viewed with more suspicion. Additionally, Eisenstadt (1956) discussed the period of youth and associated rebellious behaviour as a form of 'safety valve', where young people can get high spirits out of their system and let off some steam. This will prove functional for society later on, when they settle down as well-adjusted adults, but it also justifies the different treatment that youths will receive in society.

In terms of old age, Parsons recognised that the social and economic roles associated with adulthood (namely, childbearing and rearing, and work) are no longer performed by those in the older age group, thus the latter will lose status and importance in society because their contribution is over. Some older people may become less physically able to maintain their roles in society, specifically in the world of work.

Parsons was discussing US society, and did acknowledge that in other societies — for example, where the extended family is more important, where the role of adults is less complex, or where work takes place in family or communities — the role and status of the different age groups may differ.

Another functionalist-type view relating to the inequalities suffered by older people is put forward by Cummings and Henry (1961). Their 'disengagement theory' suggests that it is functional and inevitable that older people will begin to withdraw from the workplace and other aspects of life as their abilities and competence start to decline. Men may experience this shift more acutely, since they are traditionally more defined by their workplace role, whereas women's key family-based role will just evolve. A consequence of the withdrawal is that older people will become more distanced from evolving social norms, which can then explain differences in their experiences. Such disengagement is also functional for society because older people need to make way for the younger people coming after them.

The New Right has not focused specifically on age in discussions on inequality. However, one emphasis of New Right writers such as Charles Murray and Peter Saunders is personal responsibility and the negative impacts of over-reliance on the state to intervene. This can be applied to both old people and young people.

Murray (1989) claimed that the UK benefit system creates dependency culture, which disincentivises people to work hard and take responsibility for the consequences of their actions and decision making. Young people born into such a culture will often repeat this behaviour. Murray particularly expressed concern about teenage pregnancy and unmarried mothers, who assume that the state will provide them with a flat and an income. The fathers, often young males from similar backgrounds, do not accept the consequences of their actions or see their child as their responsibility. Youths brought up in such a culture will learn to behave in similarly 'feckless' ways, with boys becoming delinquent due to a lack of discipline and an absence of a father figure in their lives, and will repeat the same behaviour as their own absent dads. Girls will look for a father substitute and are also likely to get pregnant at a young age.

> **Knowledge check 24**
>
> How could the generational digital divide — the lack of access to and competence in digital technology found in older people — be used to support the ideas of Parsons and Cummings and Henry?

Older people could also be seen as an economic burden on the state. The New Right may question whether the state has a responsibility to support people as they age. The provision of a universal and generous state pension will disincentivise individuals from taking responsibility for their futures in terms of planning and saving for their retirement. An example of such thinking can be seen in the policies of the Conservative government under Margaret Thatcher in the 1980s, which is regarded as heavily influenced by the New Right. One of Thatcher's early moves was to abolish the link between the state pension and earnings in 1980, which led to a progressive devaluing of the state pension.

These views then suggest that inequalities faced by those in both age groups can be explained in relation to their contribution and value to society.

Evaluation of functionalist and New Right explanations

Functionalists can be challenged for underestimating the dysfunctions of age inequality. For example, social disengagement is often enforced, rather than a choice, with older people being pushed out of the workplace, for example. This can be damaging and isolating to individuals, leading to poverty and isolation. Additionally, evidence suggests that when people withdraw from the workplace, their health — both physical and mental — often starts to deteriorate, which can be costly to society and not functional at all. This also relates to New Right ideas, since cutting state pensions would leave many older people in poverty, which would have knock-on effects in terms of costs to the health and social care services, so may not in fact prove cost effective.

The functionalist view of youth is also challenged: the idea that youths rebel because society needs them to is questionable, and neo-Marxists would argue that youth rebellion is active and conscious resistance against capitalism rather than simply 'letting off steam'.

Marxist explanations

Marxists focus on the needs of capitalism when trying to explain inequality, and therefore on the value of a particular group of people in terms of their labour and the costs of a particular group of people in terms of their demands on the state. These ideas can be applied to consider the relative situations of those in both the older and the younger age groups.

Young people are an asset to the bourgeoisie, due to the energy and new skills they can provide. They can also be a cheap source of labour due to lower minimum wages and the poor pay associated with apprenticeships, which is beneficial to the capitalist system. However, young people may be less easy to control because they are subject to less ideological control and have fewer financial and personal commitments tying them to their jobs. Neo-Marxists from the Centre for Contemporary Cultural Studies (CCCS) (1972) studied the rebellious youth subcultures of the 1960s and 1970s, interpreting the deviance of this group of people as a resistance against their social class position and lack of power. Such rebellion needs to be controlled and undermined, thus the marginalisation of young people, and the denial of any rights or status, keeps them in a subservient position and neutralises their threat.

Older people may also bring benefits to the capitalist economy, for example through their willingness to take on voluntary work and to care for grandchildren with no

Exam tip

If you have studied youth subcultures in Component 1, some of the explanations for the perceptions and treatment of youths can be applied here.

monetary reward. This also allows the parents to work more efficiently and takes the burden off the state, benefiting capitalism.

However, elderly people as a group do not contribute economically, so are less significant to capitalists than working-age adults. Phillipson (1982) suggests that capitalism is about exploiting workers and consumers for profit, so older people are given little or no attention, rather they are seen as a drain on the economy. They are also less easy to exploit than workers who have families to support and mortgages to pay for; they may be less prepared to take on extra duties for no extra money. Due to years of experience, older workers are also likely to cost more, decreasing their value for employers. The perception that older workers are less competent (Ray et al. 2006) can also help explain why some employers discriminate negatively against older workers.

Phillipson (1982) argues that age is a social construction which leads to challenges in a capitalist society. For example, the capitalist mode of production allows workers to develop a limited range of skills within the division of labour, which Marx argues leads to feelings of **alienation** and limits their ability to develop as individuals. When they retire, people are told that they will be free to express themselves more fully, with all the extra time they have, and pursue their own interests. However, financial constraints mean that retirement is often an even more limiting and alienating experience, thus older people have been ejected from the labour force and discarded by a system which has no further use for them.

Phillipson also suggests that early retirement policies from the 1980s onwards affected employers' attitudes towards older workers in general. Employers increasingly started to see workers over 50 as redundant and unemployable, and to discriminate negatively in terms of recruitment, training and retirement practices, often seeing early retirement policies as an 'easy solution' for personnel management, especially in times of radical change in the global economy. This could link with the reserve army of labour.

Weberian explanations

Class, status and party

Weberians would argue that those in the older age group have a low market position (class) due to lack of earning power. Although older workers are experienced, the knowledge and skills accrued by them are undervalued and seen as out of date. The Equality Act 2010, which makes age discrimination by employers unlawful, has led to a spotlight being placed on the kinds of wording employers use when recruiting. Words such as 'dynamic' and 'flexible' are seen to demonstrate the engrained expectations held about older workers and their desirability. This attitude is more explicitly shown in the infamous quote from Mark Zuckerberg, chief executive officer (CEO) and co-founder of Facebook: 'young people are just smarter'.

Older people also have a low status in society, as they are not aspirational — we do not want to be like them because we all fear becoming old. Parkin's (1968) concept of negatively privileged status groups can thus be applied to older people, who are excluded by those in high status privileged groups via social closure. Examples include being pushed out of the workplace and under-represented in the media.

> **Knowledge check 25**
> How can the Marxist concept of the reserve army of labour be applied to both older and younger people?

> **Alienation** This concept was used by Karl Marx to describe the feelings of detachment and estrangement experienced by the proletariat arising from their lack of control and autonomy in their work.

Turner (1989) argues that the status of older people is linked to the values of the society. In Western societies which value material wealth, both older and younger people may lack status because they do not control resources or have access to wealth and thus have low earning potential. However, in societies which value knowledge and experience, old age may bring status and be a source of power. For example, in the Samburu society in Kenya the elders are the rulers and are powerful and highly respected.

Party relates to the power gained by association with others, such as membership of a group or organisation. Older people are likely to have experienced a loss of social capital and membership of organisations which are usually work-related, and are less represented in public bodies and institutions, including parliament.

Vincent (2003) argues that age stratification is an important source of inequality, and has a huge effect on life chances. He points out that experiences of age differ widely as it intersects with class, gender and ethnicity. For example, the social significance of ageing can vary hugely for men and women, those from different ethnic groups may have different cultural attitudes towards elderly family members, and social class and poverty have a huge impact on the experience of old age. This links to Weberian ideas about relative sources of status. Townsend (1981) supports the view that age intersects with social class. He argues that it is those from the working class who have little money during their working lives to contribute to a pension, and so rely on the state, who end up in poverty in old age — so the experience of old age is directly related to social class (market position). The state pension is inadequate and does not reward the full contribution made by many hardworking people throughout their lives (low status once retired).

This Weberian analysis — using class, status and party — could also be applied to youth. Younger people have a lower class or market position (due to lack of skills and experience), low status (young people are often ignored, stereotypes and dismissed by wider adult society) and low party (lower social capital, fewer contacts and connections, less likely to be part of trade unions and so on.)

The dual labour market theory can also be related to age — both elderly and young workers are likely to be concentrated in the secondary labour market, with temporary, waged and low-paid work.

Because Weber had a more micro approach, Weberian explanations could be supported by those which are more interactionist in nature. Micro views tend to place particular emphasis on the social construction of age and the meanings associated with different age groups, but place less emphasis on power structures than Marxists. They argue that the categorisation of the life course into stages is artificial, and socially constructed, and although ageing is a biological process, ideas about when childhood or adulthood begin and end are changeable between societies and times.

One notable micro analysis of age inequality comes from Hockey and James (1993). They link old age and childhood, and argue they are socially constructed in a similar way. In Western societies, 'personhood' or citizenship (being accepted as a full member of society) relates to your status as a competent adult. It can be seen that children and elderly people, but also those with disabilities and even potentially those from minority ethnic groups or women, lack this status of 'personhood'.

Knowledge check 26

Why are young and older workers more likely to be concentrated in the secondary labour market?

Exam tip

Some Weberian views on age can be related to Marxist views, since ideas about older or younger people lacking status can be linked to their value to capitalism. As long as you are careful not to confuse them, you could use some to support others in an essay. However, always make it clear which theory a sociologist comes from, or avoid labelling them if you are unsure: 'Smith's ideas can support Marxists when he says that…'.

Hockey and James argue that older people are seen in a similar way to children — having lost their 'personhood' status. Terms such as 'gaga' are used (relating to baby noises), and elderly individuals are also seen as helpless, vulnerable, dependent and needing care. Hockey and James use the concept 'infantilisation' to describe this. In their research in a residential home, they reported that the clients were treated like children: not allowed to keep their own money, lacking powers to make decisions, lacking privacy, and assumed to be innocent and compliant. Although these practices may have been justified as meeting the needs of the residents, Hockey and James argue that they were not based on medical needs and had the potential to create a self-fulfilling prophecy.

Evaluation of Marxist and Weberian explanations

A positive point about Weberian explanations, and Marxist ones to an extent, is the acknowledgement of links with other sources of inequality: class, ethnicity and so on. Feminists, however, would place even more emphasis on gender.

Previous criticisms of the Marxist concept of the reserve army of labour and the Weberian dual labour market can be applied to their use in explaining age inequality as well.

Postmodernists would argue that age is more fluid than these theories suggest and has ceased to be a significant source of inequality. As the population ages, more and more older people continue to work and occupy powerful positions in society, and thus ideas of ageing are changing. For example, Featherstone and Hepworth (1993) argue that the life-course has been deconstructed, with less separation between childhood, adulthood and old age, and more choices for people at various stages of their lives.

Feminist explanations

Feminists have considered issues of age inequality and how they relate to women. The prominent feminist writer Simone de Beauvoir (1972) suggested that ageing has a greater impact on men than women. While recognising that women tend to live longer and risk an isolated and solitary old age, she argued that the transition to retirement has a greater impact on men since their identities are so wrapped up in the role of breadwinner. Women, on the other hand, are not 'thrown into total idleness', given their continuing domestic role. She acknowledges, though, that as children grow up and leave home this can have a significant impact on women and their identities as mothers.

However, other feminists have tended to argue that ageing has a more negative impact on women than men. While agreeing that men's status is linked to employment, Itzin (1990) points out that women's status is linked to reproduction, and that patriarchal societies tend to devalue women once the menopause sets in. This also links to the idea that women are judged more on appearance and attractiveness than men and, given that attractiveness is synonymous with youth in Western societies, women are under pressure to fight the signs of ageing and older women are marginalised.

Gannon (1999) also argues that the process of ageing is seen differently in men and women, and women's ageing is seen from a male, androcentric perspective. A key example is the way the menopause is viewed — as a 'disease' needing treatment and as a loss of femininity — and is colloquially referred to as the 'change' as if a woman is changing into something else. Males also experience changes in hormone levels as they

> **Exam tip**
>
> If you are applying related views to expand and support a theoretical explanation named in an exam question, make sure you show how and why they are related and relevant.

> **Knowledge check 27**
>
> Give examples from the media and elsewhere of older women being marginalised or becoming less visible.

age, but this is not focused on in the same way. These views can be supported with evidence that older women have been viewed with suspicion throughout history — persecuted as scolds and witches, for example — and generally seen as a threat to male power, especially if they lived alone and did not submit to the control of a man.

Walby (1990) identified the 'dual systems' of patriarchy and capitalism as oppressive forces, and later added in racism in her triple systems theory (1999). However, more recently (2012) she has developed her ideas further to fully embrace the concept of **intersectionality**, which recognises the complex interplay between different forms of social inequality including class, gender, ethnicity, religion, sexuality, nationality and, importantly, age. Arguing that patriarchy continues to impact on the lives of all women, she suggests that the restrictions of patriarchy for older women are even greater.

The link between women and attractiveness may also be seen to disadvantage younger women, who may be subject to sexualisation and harassment, and judged purely on appearance and not on achievements. Many feminist studies on the pressures on young women relating to their appearance have been conducted, such as Wolf's work *The Beauty Myth* (1990), in which she discusses how images of beauty and attractiveness are used to oppress and control women. This may particularly apply to younger women, but also pressurise older women to try and maintain their youthful appearance. Young women and girls are also subject to more control by their peers (Lees 1997) and their parents (Smart 1976), and also by judgements on their behaviour via the media, according to Heidensohn (2000).

Oakley (2004) considered society's perception of childhood and its relationship to women, arguing that there are similarities in the way that women and children are treated in society. For example, both women and children are seen as 'minority groups', and as physically and culturally different from the 'norm' (adult men). Neither group is automatically given full rights. Rights to make decisions, to live independently, to vote and so on have been hard won by women, and children are still denied many rights. Historically, the justification for denying women such rights related to their perceived equivalence with children: weaker, in need of protection and less intellectually developed. Therefore, both have traditionally been seen as in need of 'protection' and incapable of knowing what is good for them, which has been used to justify some of the denial of rights.

Oakley also says that comparing women and children 'conveys a picture of mutual dependence and interdependence and mutual oppression', suggesting that children are a source of women's oppression, but also that women, as mothers, will often be part of the social control of children.

Evaluation of feminist explanations

Feminists are challenged for their reductionism. In a similar way to Marxists with social class, feminists tend to reduce inequalities to gender-related explanations, always focusing on patriarchy and not addressing age as an aspect of inequality in its own right, which also impacts on men. Although Walby and others do consider intersectionality, gender is always at the heart of their analyses, with other aspects, including age, being reduced to one among many intersecting issues affecting women.

Intersectionality

Generally related to gender and feminism, this term refers to the recognition of the intersections between gender, social class, ethnicity, age and so on, suggesting that women or men cannot be thought of as one homogeneous group.

Exam tip

Remember the importance of evaluation in 40-mark essays. Learn the specific evaluation points suggested here but also use opposing theories to evaluate. Show *how* and *why* the other views would differ from and criticise the main view. However, avoid juxtaposition, which is simply describing alternative theories with no attempt to challenge the view in the question.

Content Guidance

> **Summary: age inequality**
>
> - Older people often experience prejudice and discrimination, known as ageism, particularly in terms of the workplace and health, though also in other aspects of society including media representation.
> - Children and young people are also relatively powerless groups and consequently also experience specific types of prejudice and discrimination. Young workers are subject to particular discrimination in the workplace.
> - Functionalist explanations for age inequality focus on the functional benefit to society of splitting people into different age groups, and the role and contribution each age group makes. The New Right would support this and consider how older and younger people may be a particular burden on the state.
> - Weberian ideas of market position and status are particularly relevant to the ways in which older and younger people are valued and perceived in Western societies. More micro views relating to the status of personhood and labelling are also relevant.
> - The main focus of Marxist explanations for age inequality is the benefit to capitalist society of different age groups in terms of their value as workers. Feminists would relate this to older women in particular, suggesting that it is patriarchy, rather than capitalism, which devalues older women as unattractive and thus having no value.

Questions & Answers

How to use this section

In this section you will find examples of three A-level papers. Each question part is followed by a brief analysis of what to watch out for when answering it. At the end of the question and analysis section, an A/A*-grade student answer is given for each question, with commentary throughout indicating where credit is due.

Read each question carefully and try to answer it in full, or at least make notes on how you would answer it, before reading the student answer and comments. Remember that there is no single way of answering an exam question — high marks can be gained taking different approaches. However, the example answers and comments should help to show you the kinds of approach that would do well and some of the pitfalls to avoid.

As a general point, you should always read the whole question before starting to write. When you come to a question that is based on a source, study the source carefully before you start writing, as it will contain material that is essential to answering the question.

The student answers are accompanied by comments. The comments tell you what it is that enables the student to score so highly and where or why they miss out on any marks.

Examinable skills

OCR Sociology examination papers are designed to test certain defined skills. These skills are expressed as assessment objectives (AOs). There are three AOs and it is important that you know what these are and what you have to be able to do in an exam to show your ability in each.

Assessment objective 1

Demonstrate knowledge and understanding of:
- **sociological theories, studies, theorists, concepts and empirical data**
- **sociological research methods**

Your answers must demonstrate clearly to the examiners that your knowledge is accurate and appropriate to the topic being discussed and that you have a clear understanding of it. It is not enough simply to reproduce knowledge learned by rote — you must be able to use your knowledge of concepts, sociological studies, empirical evidence and sociological theories in a meaningful and logical way to address the specific question set.

Questions & Answers

Assessment objective 2

Apply sociological theories, concepts, evidence and research methods to a range of issues.

This means that you must be able to demonstrate the ability to address the question throughout your response by consistently applying relevant sociological evidence (including concepts, studies, theories and/or statistics).

The questions in Section A, which are specifically focused on sociological research methods, will instruct you to use one or other of the two sources. You must read and analyse these sources carefully and use them in your answer. However, 'applying' the material does not mean simply copying it from the source and leaving it to speak for itself. You will need to show your understanding of the material by doing something with it, such using it to illustrate a strength or weakness of a method or approach to research and to give context to your answer.

Application in Section B questions is assessed on your ability to select and link appropriate sociological evidence to the precise question asked. Make sure you stay focused on the question you have been given, and do not be tempted to veer off into other aspects of inequalities or theories of inequality, even if you feel more confident about them or want to show off your other knowledge. You will only be credited for knowledge which is relevant!

Assessment objective 3

Analyse and evaluate sociological theories, concepts, evidence and research methods in order to:
- **present arguments**
- **make judgements**
- **draw conclusions**

The skill of *evaluation* is shown by the ability to identify the strengths and weaknesses or limitations of any sociological material. It is not sufficient, however, simply to list the strengths or limitations of something — you need to be able to say *why* something is considered a strength or otherwise, and sometimes you will need to state *who* claims that this is a strength or weakness. Depending on what it is you are discussing, you may be able to reach a credible and supported conclusion about the relative merits or otherwise of something. This means that it should be based on the sociological arguments and evidence that you have presented during your answer. Merely presenting opposing explanations does not constitute analysis or evaluation — ensure you make some comparison and show why these opposing views would challenge the main view in the question.

Weighting of assessment objectives

In the exam papers, each AO is given a particular weighting, which indicates its relative importance to the overall mark gained. You can find out the breakdown of AO weightings for each question in the mark schemes for past papers, which are on the OCR website (www.ocr.org.uk), and they are given below after each question. These stay constant every year.

Command words

Ofqual, the body that sets the criteria for all GCE Sociology specifications, has an approved list of 'command words' that are used in exam questions. The following are some of the most commonly used, but this list is not exhaustive and occasionally other, similar words or phrases may be used instead. It is worth learning what these command words mean, to ensure that you give an appropriate response.

Summarise Present some conclusions that can be drawn from the data provided.

Define Give the meaning of something.

Explain Describe the purposes or uses of something, give reasons for it or present the main arguments supporting a method, view or theory.

Describe/Outline Give the main characteristics of a concept or sociological view, or present evidence relating to or supporting a position.

Outline and explain Give the main characteristics of a sociological view and develop these by referencing studies and using examples.

Using the source and your wider sociological knowledge, explain... Draw on the material provided and develop it using your own knowledge to answer the question.

Evaluate/Discuss/Assess Explain and develop support for but also criticisms of the view, and/or use alternative views to challenge and highlight weaknesses in the view.

■ The A-level examination

The topic of 'Researching and understanding social inequalities' is examined on Paper 2 of the A-level examination, which is organised into two sections.

Section A, which focuses on 'Research methods and researching social inequalities', contains two sources. Source A is likely to depict research data on some aspect of social inequality, while Source B is likely to contain a detailed description of a particular piece of research, how it was carried out and its findings. Section A includes four compulsory questions worth 4, 6, 10 and 25 marks respectively. You will be instructed to use Source A or Source B to help you answer these questions, although your responses to questions 2, 3 and 4 will also require you to use 'your wider sociological knowledge'. Section A questions add up to 45 marks altogether.

Section B is 'Understanding social inequalities' and will contain two compulsory questions, worth 20 and 40 marks, adding up to 60 marks altogether.

The exam lasts for 2 hours 15 minutes, carries 105 marks and is worth 35% of the A-level qualification. It is worth spending about 60 minutes on Section A (including time to carefully read both sources) and 75 minutes on Section B.

Questions & Answers

■ Example 1 questions

Section A

Read the source material and answer **all** the questions in Section A.

Source A

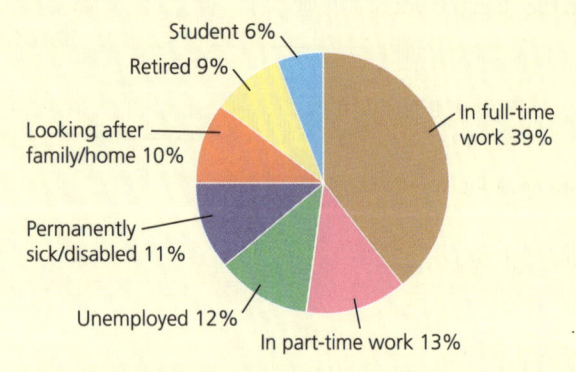

Student 6%
Retired 9%
Looking after family/home 10%
Permanently sick/disabled 11%
Unemployed 12%
In part-time work 13%
In full-time work 39%

Deprived adults by employment status
Source: PSE UK 2012

> To operationalise the concept of 'deprived' the researchers first created a list of 'necessities' based on a separate attitudes survey. An item or activity was defined as a 'necessity' when over 50% of respondents agreed that it was.
>
> Then, in a living standards questionnaire, a different sample of adults was asked which of these necessities they had. An adult lacking three or more necessities because they could not afford them was defined as 'deprived'.
>
> The sample size for the living standards questionnaire was 5,193 households (4,205 in Britain and 988 in Northern Ireland) in which 12,097 people were living (9,786 in Britain and 2,311 in Northern Ireland).

Source B

Media representations of young, black males

> Kerry Moore, John Jewell and Stephen Cushion carried out a study which sought to explore whether the news media present negative images or stereotypes of black young men and boys, and how such images are constructed. They employed a mixed methods approach, including both quantitative and qualitative content analyses and semi-structured interviews.
>
> The content analysis was based on a sample of all UK daily and weekend national newspapers, a selection of regional newspapers and a range of television and radio news bulletins. They monitored the media for sixteen weeks in total, evenly spaced over eighteen months in 2008–9.
>
> The analyses included a number of different categories for examining the patterns of coverage. These included within each media type: the volume

of coverage; the prominence of news; when stories occurred; sources quoted and the story subject.

The researchers then conducted a more qualitative analysis of a range of mainstream print and broadcast news media, with the aim of assessing how and why certain ideas were constructed in the coverage and the social meaning and significance of these constructions.

Finally, they conducted a series of semi-structured interviews with journalists and editors working within or across a range of news media organisations in Britain.

Moore et al. identified that black young men and boys are regularly associated with negative news values. While young men and boys in general were regularly reported in relation to negative news values (just over 4 in 10 stories being crime-related), close to 7 in 10 stories of black young men and boys related in some form to crime. In the mainstream news media little context or explanation was provided in news reports regarding why crime may have been committed. Crimes such as knife attacks and murders were often represented as irrational, senseless acts of violence, or motivated by trivial petty rows or gang rivalries. Very little commentary concerning possible systemic or structural factors surrounding the crime was evident.

The journalists and editors were aware of press guidelines concerning the reporting of 'race' or ethnic identity, and they asserted that they did not consider the black identity of perpetrators to be relevant to the news value of a story. However, in reflecting upon their practice in reporting stories featuring black young men and boys, journalists and editors acknowledged that coverage tends to be predominantly negative. Several voiced concern about what they saw as a problematic image associating young black males with gangs and violent crime. Interview respondents also highlighted that there are still comparatively few people working in mainstream journalism from a black or minority ethnic background.

Adapted from Kerry Moore, John Jewell and Stephen Cushion (2011) 'Media representations of black young men and boys', the REACH media monitoring project; used with permission

Question 1

Summarise the data shown in the pie chart in Source A. 4 marks (AO2)

> Make sure you support patterns you identify with data, and make comparisons between different categories. Make two clear points.

Question 2

With reference to Source B, explain two reasons why some sociologists use mixed methods when conducting research. 6 marks (AO1: 2 marks; AO2: 4 marks)

> Don't forget to illustrate with reference to Source B.

Questions & Answers

Question 3

With reference to Source A, explain **one** strength and **one** weakness of the way the concept of 'deprived' was operationalised.   10 marks (AO2: 4 marks; AO3: 6 marks)

> Make sure each strength and weakness is detailed and refers to Source A.

Question 4

Using Source B and your wider sociological knowledge, assess the usefulness of content analysis for investigating the representations of black young men and boys.   25 marks (AO1: 5 marks; AO2: 5 marks; AO3: 15 marks)

> Describe the method and explain how it works in practice before describing and assessing its strengths and weaknesses. Use specific examples from Source B to illustrate your points, aiming for at least two strengths and two weaknesses.

Section B

Answer **all** the questions in Section B.

Question 5

Outline ways in which working-class people are disadvantaged in UK society.   20 marks (AO1: 12 marks; AO2: 8 marks)

> Make sure you focus on 'disadvantage', so make comparisons with other classes. Also try to refer to a range of areas of social life where life chances are affected, rather than to just one.

Question 6

Evaluate the view that ethnic inequalities are caused by the structure of society rather than the culture of individuals.   40 marks (AO1: 16 marks; AO2: 8 marks; AO3: 16 marks)

> Consider which theories tend to blame the structure of society for ethnic inequalities and which blame individuals' culture to ensure you get the right focus here.

Student answer

1   Source A shows which adults are more likely to be deprived based on their employment status.

The largest proportion of adults who are deprived are those who are working full-time, at 39%. This is three times higher than the next nearest category, which is those working part-time, and both the working categories are higher than the other categories.

In terms of the adults who are not working, the most likely deprived adults are those who are unemployed, at 12% compared to the lowest group which is students at 6% — double the percentage.

> These data are quite simple, so there is a danger of just reproducing the figures. Always try to make some kind of comparison — which this answer does well, comparing proportions of different groups with specific data.
> **4/4 marks awarded**

Example 1 questions

Student answer

2 Mixed methods means using more than one research method in a study. Sometimes this is a combination of qualitative and quantitative methods and may be used to achieve triangulation. Qualitative methods may give the researcher validity, due to their depth, but they may not be seen as reliable, because they cannot be repeated. On the other hand, quantitative methods are more standardised and reliable, but may not be so valid, since they do not give a true picture. Using both will give the researcher the best of both worlds.

Another reason for using mixed methods is to get a complete picture. Methodological pluralism allows a researcher to get a fuller picture which is relevant in Source B because the content analysis shows what is happening in the media, and the interviews with the journalists show why it is happening, which is a good reason to use mixed methods in this case.

> These two points are good, with use of concepts, and well explained — 2 marks for AO1. The first point has no reference to Source B unfortunately, losing 2 of the possible 4 marks for AO2.
> **4/6 marks awarded**

Student answer

3 One strength was that by operationalising 'deprived' with the indicators of necessities they lacked, this means every participant would understand it in the same way, so it is clearly measurable. If they just asked 'are you deprived?' everyone may interpret this in different ways, so the data would not be reliable, since they could not be replicated and compared. Positivists would value this method of operationalising concepts, since it makes the research more scientific and objective.

One weakness is that it relies on what the people in the first survey defined as necessities, which might vary between different people and over time. Interpretivists would argue that each person would have a different definition, so the concepts should be explored through unstructured interviews rather than operationalised in this quantitative way, since it would be more valid then.

> This is a good answer which demonstrates clear understanding of the question and uses the information in the source well to help explain it. Students often struggle to understand and explain the process of operationalising concepts so this example should be helpful.
> **10/10 marks awarded**

Questions & Answers

Student answer

4 Content analysis is a method used to analyse qualitative secondary data, usually media content. If a researcher is investigating how a group is represented in the media, it is the best technique, because it involves actually looking at the media content and analysing the representations, whereas doing questionnaires or interviews would just tell you what people think about the representations. Therefore, it is the best method to gain valid data about what the media actually do. In Source B it shows how young black males are actually represented in the news, by analysing newspapers, television and radio news bulletins over eighteen months in 2008–9.

> A clear explanation of the method is given, which is always a useful way to start. There is not much to this point, but it links in validity and refers to the source. Try to extend your points to ensure they are fully developed.

Another advantage of using content analysis is that it can be done in either a qualitative or quantitative way or both, though it is usually quantitative. In Source B they did both. By having various categories to look for they could get reliable, quantitative data, since they could be repeated over another time period, which positivists would like. For example, they found that 7 out of 10 stories about black males related to crime. They could repeat this to check if this figure was reliable. However, they also interpreted the media content, by looking at the prominence of the stories and the sources quoted. This would be more valued by interpretivists since it would give more validity and depth.

A weakness of content analysis is that it relies on the researchers' interpretations of the categories, and therefore may be subjective and biased. This means that positivists would criticise it. For example, if a story was on another topic, such as rap music, but mentioned crime, how would this be categorised? This creates a problem of researcher imposition and means the data are not reliable.

> This weakness is quite brief, but does use theory and the concept of reliability accurately.

Another weakness is that a lot of content analysis is quantitative and just involves counting stories. This does not give the context behind the stories and is turning qualitative content into quantitative data, so will lack validity. Interpretivists would argue that a qualitative approach involving semiological analysis, where the connotations are looked at, is more valid. In studying black youths' representation in the media, a story about crime could be positive or negative, so a statistic like '7 out of 10 stories about black males related to crime' does not give a valid picture since these stories may have different connotations.

Overall, content analysis is the best method to look at media content, especially if it combines both quantitative and qualitative analysis.

> A concise but accurate answer, which is well linked to the source. It loses a few marks for the slight lack of development in places.
> **22/25 marks awarded**

Example 1 questions

Student answer

5   People from working-class backgrounds experience many disadvantages compared to their middle-class and upper-class counterparts. One area this can be seen is in education. Double the proportion of middle-class pupils achieve good GCSE grades compared to working-class pupils. This could relate to issues of teacher labelling according to interactionists such as Becker, who argues that teachers have an 'ideal pupil' in their head, who is middle-class. This may lead working-class pupils to give up on academic achievement and form anti-school subcultures. Reay argues that this is understandable, since education is a game working-class pupils cannot win.

This disadvantage continues into higher education, since Bourdieu argues that for working-class pupils, being at university is often like being a 'fish out of water'. Additionally, high tuition fees put many working-class students off university according to Callender and Jackson, since they experience debt aversion and do not feel that university is worth it. This disadvantages them in comparison to middle- and upper-class students.

The area of education is clearly identified and two separate points are made, both supported with evidence.

Another area is the workplace. The Sutton Trust shows that those who went to state schools are disadvantaged in accessing the top professions, such as law and journalism, compared to those who went to private schools. In 2016 they found that 74% of top judges went to Oxford or Cambridge and were privately educated, even though only 7% of the population are privately education and only 1% go to Oxbridge.

Using statistics is fine as evidence, but make sure you say who found the statistics and when, and that they are accurate, as this student does here.

This also links to disadvantage in terms of income. Working-class people are more likely to be on minimum wage jobs, which Wadsworth found is not enough to support a family so many have to take on a second job. In contrast, children from middle-class backgrounds have a 2.5 greater chance of gaining a professional job themselves. The Social Mobility Commission found that there is a class pay gap of over £2,000 per year, even when people have the same qualifications and are in the same types of occupations, disadvantaging those from working-class backgrounds.

A final area of disadvantage is in terms of health. Working-class people are more likely to die than middle-class people at both ends of their life. 3,500 babies born into working-class families die each year who would survive if they had the same chances of survival as middle-class babies. Working-class people also die earlier with around a 7-year life expectancy gap, which rises to up to 25 years in parts of London. This is backed up by Wilkinson and Pickett's evidence that working-class people suffer more from lifestyle-related conditions such as cancer, stroke and heart disease, which can lead to premature death.

The statistics here are less specific, but there is other evidence as well.

A range of three areas is covered, with detailed points for each, and the focus back on how this evidence shows working-class disadvantage in comparison to other classes is made well throughout. This response would get full marks.
20/20 marks awarded

Researching and understanding social inequalities   77

Questions & Answers

Student answer

6   The inequalities experienced by some ethnic groups, especially minority ones, in the UK can either be blamed on the ethnic groups themselves and their culture, or blamed on structural issues in society. Theories which support the structural explanations include Marxist and Weberian ones.

Marxists argue that inequalities are created by and benefit capitalism. Ethnic inequalities are related to social class, and most minority ethnic groups who are disadvantaged are also working class. Therefore, Marx's ideas about how the proletariat are exploited by the bourgeoisie in order to make profit for the bourgeoisie can be applied to explain ethnic inequality as well. Minority ethnic workers are often in lower paid and lower status jobs, and not paid the full value of their labour, with the surplus value being taken as profit by their employers. Castles and Kosack argue that in the 1950s and 1960s, most new immigrants were concentrated in low-skilled and low-paid jobs and served as a reserve army of labour to ensure that the white British workers did not have too much power over their employers. Therefore, the capitalist structure of society can explain the inequalities which these workers faced.

Castles and Kosack also argue that it benefits the bourgeoisie to create racism and divisions within the working class. This will prevent them developing class consciousness and rising up against the bourgeoisie. It also gives the white workers, who are also exploited, someone to blame for their problems. This scapegoating is encouraged by those in power, as Hall showed in his study where black youths were stereotyped as muggers in order to distract the white working class from the economic problems in society, and give them someone to blame. These ideas show how it is the capitalist structure of society which causes and maintains racial divisions and inequalities.

Marxists can be criticised as being unrealistic and outdated. Many people from ethnic minorities are not disadvantaged and the white working class are much more disadvantaged than those from Indian and Chinese backgrounds, suggesting that the argument of Castles and Kosack is too simplistic. Also, by arguing that racism is all just about capitalism and the bourgeoisie, Marxists are trivialising racism and racial inequalities, which are important in their own right.

Functionalists argue that racial inequalities are caused by the culture of different ethnic groups. Patterson came up with the host–immigrant model. She argues that the majority ethnic population in a country are like the hosts, and when immigrants come it feels strange because they have different norms and

> Although an introduction is not always necessary, in a question like this it is useful to identify which theories support the view in the question.

> These two Marxist paragraphs are well explained and focused on the question, with evidence in support.

> This evaluation is creditable, but to be seen as fully developed it needs supporting with some evidence. Try to use another theory, a named sociologist or some evidence to support any criticisms you make.

Example 1 questions

values, like a stranger staying in your house. This will create tensions and can lead to racial discrimination. However, if the immigrants assimilate to the host culture and learn their norms and values then racial inequalities will be overcome.

Weberians would also agree with the view that ethnic inequalities are caused by the structure of society focusing on issues of hierarchy and status within our society, since they see ethnicity as an aspect of status and argue that those from minority ethnic groups have lower status. In order to maintain their privileged status, Parkin argues that the white majority operates social closure and exclusionary tactics against minority ethnic groups, who are negatively privileged status groups. Therefore the competitive structure of society in terms of status and the privilege it brings causes ethnic inequalities. Weberians Rex and Tomlinson would agree with this and discuss the black underclass which is isolated and socially excluded in terms of class and race.

These ideas are challenged by the New Right and Charles Murray. When he discusses the underclass he sees them as culturally inferior, unlike Rex and Tomlinson, so while he agrees that some minority ethnic groups are over-represented in the underclass, he puts the blame on their culture rather than the structure of society. One particular concern to Murray is unmarried mothers who have children they cannot afford without the support of the father. He says this is common in African Americans, and in the UK has been linked by some, such as Sewell, to African Caribbean culture. According to Murray, boys growing up in these households will lack a male role model, lack discipline and not develop the right work ethic, therefore their culture is responsible for their inequality, rather than the structure of society.

In conclusion, Marxists and Weberians think ethnic inequality is caused by the structure of society, whereas functionalists and the New Right disagree.

This paragraph gains little credit since it is juxtaposition. It does not attempt to evaluate or challenge the view in the question so it is only implicitly relevant. You could turn this into an evaluative paragraph by highlighting how Patterson's ideas differ from those of the Marxists, with their focus on culture rather than the structure of society. Make sure you never just present alternative views without using them to explicitly evaluate the view in the question.

This evaluative paragraph shows the difference between juxtaposition and full evaluation, since this time the student uses it to challenge the previous point directly and links it back clearly to the view in the question.

This essay has some good content, and applies the knowledge used effectively to the question. However, it lacks enough range of knowledge, presenting two Marxist points and one Weberian one. To reach the top level in a 40-mark essay, at least four developed points are needed. This essay could have applied black feminism, for example, or additional ideas from Weberian or Marxist perspectives. So this answer achieves 12 marks for AO1 and 6 marks for AO2, since there is not a full range of evidence selected and applied to the question. The evaluation is also lacking in range. Some is underdeveloped and some merely juxtaposed. There is a conclusion, but this adds little — try to make a judgement based on the evidence discussed rather than just sum up or repeat the differing views. For this reason, 9 marks are gained for AO3.
27/40 marks awarded

Overall, the student scores 87 marks out of a possible 105 for this paper.

Questions & Answers

■ Example 2 questions

Section A

Read the source material and answer **all** the questions in Section A.

Source A

Percentage of households by combined economic status UK, October to December, 2004, 2017 and 2018

	All households			Excluding student households		
	October to December 2004 (%)	October to December 2017 (%)	October to December 2018 (%)	October to December 2004 (%)	October to December 2017 (%)	October to December 2018 (%)
Working households	56.4	58.8	59.2	56.8	59.2	59.6
Mixed households	26.1	26.8	27.1	26.1	26.8	27.0
Workless households	17.5	14.4	13.7	17.1	14.0	13.4

Source: Office for National Statistics, Household Labour Force Survey 2019

Source B

Experiences of lad culture in higher education

Alison Phipps and Isabel Young undertook qualitative research focused on women students' experiences in higher education as part of a larger piece of research commissioned by the National Union of Students. The research aimed to examine the phenomenon of 'lad culture', and women students' encounters with it in the context of higher education.

Phipps and Young gathered primary data from interviews and focus groups with 40 women students from England and Scotland. In order to select their sample, the researchers contacted higher education institutions and student groups across the UK, using 'gatekeepers' such as students' unions, sports groups and societies, media such as student newspapers, Facebook and Twitter and also snowballing from contacts with individual participants. The majority were undergraduate students aged between 18 and 25, although some were postgraduates and two were over 30. Almost 80 percent identified as heterosexual, and the remainder reported a variety of different sexual orientations. Most defined their ethnicity as 'white British', and described themselves as middle class, although there were a number of other ethnicities and class positions represented. Six participants identified as disabled.

Four focus groups were conducted with 19 students in total, in major cities in England and Scotland. Each group lasted approximately 90 minutes and had between four and six participants, who often already knew each other, and were encouraged to share their experiences and ideas on a variety of different topics in a semi-structured format. The remaining 21 participants took part in semi-structured interviews, which were useful in terms of exploring issues in more depth and allowing each woman space for her own experiences and voice. Questions were adapted to suit the needs of participants, for instance by shortening the discussion in some areas in order to focus more intensively on others. The interviews were mostly conducted in person or over Skype, and lasted around an hour.

The researchers adopted a feminist approach to the research, viewing the participants as collaborators and attempting to establish a friendly rapport. Due to the potentially sensitive nature of some of the topics covered, following appropriate ethics procedures was extremely important. Participants were given full information about the research prior to taking part, participation was voluntary, they had a right to withdraw, and confidentiality and anonymity were ensured. The researchers also developed a process for signposting any participants to support services if necessary (although these were not used). They responded openly to any questions about their intentions and methods, and underwent a continual process of reflexivity throughout the study.

The findings indicated that the women students defined 'campus culture' as largely located in the social side of university life, led by undergraduates and shaped by alcohol. Campus cultures were also defined as gendered, and strongly connected with, if not inseparable from, 'lad culture'. 'Lad culture' was seen as a 'pack' mentality evident in activities such as sport and heavy alcohol consumption, and 'banter' which was often sexist, misogynist and homophobic. It was also thought to be sexualised and seen as involving the objectification of women. Participants also felt that 'lad culture' had infiltrated their personal lives through misogynist jokes and 'banter' and sexual values which made it difficult to begin and sustain committed relationships. Stories of sexual harassment and molestation were common, and there were also accounts of sexual violence.

Source: Adapted from Alison Phipps and Isabel Young (2012) '"That's what *she* said": Women students' experiences of lad culture in higher education', Centre for Gender Studies, University of Sussex, in association with the NUS; used with permission

Questions & Answers

Question 1

Summarise two patterns or trends shown in the data in Source A.   4 marks (AO2)

> Make two different, comparative points, and support them with actual data.

Question 2

With reference to Source B, explain **two** reasons why ethical issues are important when studying sensitive subjects.   6 marks (AO1: 2 marks; AO2: 4 marks)

> Make your two points clear and separate, and illustrate each with reference to Source B.

Question 3

With reference to Source A, explain **one** strength and **one** weakness of using official statistics to study households and work.   10 marks (AO2: 4 marks; AO3: 6 marks)

> Make sure each strength and weakness is detailed and is linked to the context of households and work, using the statistics in Source A to illustrate each point.

Question 4

Using Source B and your wider sociological knowledge, explain and evaluate the usefulness of semi-structured interviews for investigating the existence of 'lad culture' in higher education.   25 marks (AO1: 5 marks; AO2: 5 marks; AO3: 15 marks)

> Aim to explain at least two strengths and two weaknesses of the method, using methodological concepts and theory in your discussion. Also aim to link all points to the context — in this case the existence of 'lad culture' in HE — and illustrate with references to Source B.

Section B

Answer **all** the questions in Section B.

Question 5

Outline ways in which gender can impact on an individual's life chances in the contemporary UK.   20 marks (AO1: 12 marks; AO2: 8 marks)

> Aim to refer to some different areas of social life to avoid your response being narrow or repetitive, and include supporting evidence throughout. Both male and female life chances can be included. Try to include at least four different points.

Question 6

Assess Weberian explanations of age inequalities. 40 marks (AO1: 16 marks; AO2: 8 marks; AO3: 16 marks)

> Make sure you focus on Weberian views in the most detail, applying them to inequalities experienced by younger and/or older people. Other theories can be used, but only to directly evaluate Weberian explanations — avoid juxtaposition.

Student answer

1 One pattern shown in the data is that there are significantly more working households compared to workless or mixed households, across all years and household types. For example, 59.2% of households were defined as 'working' in December 2018, whereas only 27.1% were 'mixed' and 13.7% were 'workless'.

One trend shown is that the percentage of workless households is decreasing. In 2004 17.5% of all households were defined as 'workless', and 17.1% of households when student households were excluded were workless. However, by 2018, these percentages had gone done to 13.7% and 13.4 % respectively, a decrease of just less than 4% in both cases.

> The student makes two clear and different points, correctly identifying them as either a pattern or a trend, and quoting accurate statistics from the source to support each one, making comparisons.
> **4/4 marks awarded**

Student answer

2 Ethical issues refer to concerns about whether the research process is acceptable, in terms of its conduct and impact on the participants. All researchers should stick to ethical guidelines, such as those given by the British Sociological Association.

One reason why it is important when studying sensitive subjects is that issues of confidentiality and anonymity need to be considered to protect the participants. In Source B the interviews may involve discussions of a sexual nature, and possibly descriptions of embarrassing events, so it is important the participants feel safe and that their details will not be published.

A second reason is to protect the participants from any emotional or psychological harm or upset. If a woman had been sexually assaulted, then discussing this in an interview may bring back bad memories and cause upset. To address this issue the researchers in Source B signposted support services for participants and also established a rapport so the participants did not feel threatened.

> The first paragraph demonstrates good knowledge of ethical issues and then two clear points are identified and linked well to the source.
> **6/6 marks awarded**

Questions & Answers

Student answer

3   A strength of using official statistics is that they are conducted on a large scale and produce a lot of representative quantitative data, usually about the whole country. Positivists would value this as they take a macro approach to research and want to identify large-scale patterns and trends, such as those about work and households.

A weakness of official statistics is that they are secondary data, produced on behalf of the government. This means the researcher has no control over the way the data are collected which might affect their validity.

This is an accurate description of a strength and a weakness of official statistics, but the weakness is underdeveloped. The student does not really explain the implications of the lack of control of the data, or demonstrate their understanding of the concept of validity and why this may be an issue. This loses AO3 marks since the understanding of the strength and/or weakness are credited as evaluation in this question, and both need to be fully explained and supported with evidence. Additionally, each point is not fully linked to the context of the question — the study of households and work — or linked to Source A. The first point does pay lip service to 'work and households' but gives no indication of why this is particularly relevant, and the second point makes no reference at all, losing AO2 marks. The student is awarded 1 out of 4 marks for AO2 (one lip service only) and 4 out of 6 marks for AO3 (one developed point, using evidence, and one underdeveloped).

5/10 marks awarded

Student answer

4   Semi-structured interviews involve some standard, open-ended questions being asked, but then the researcher can ask follow-up questions or expand on certain areas, depending on the answers they get, so each interview is unique. This is referred to in Source B, as it points out that the questions were adapted and the discussion was shortened in some areas and more intense in others. This is a strength, according to interpretivists, since they want to get detailed, qualitative data which give a true picture, so is high in validity. Since all the women's experiences of lad culture would differ, allowing this flexibility would give much more personal and valid data, and make the women feel they were being listened to.

Semi-structured interviews are ideal for studying a topic such as women's experiences of lad culture, because they can be carried out in a relaxed setting, and a rapport can be built up, which allows for more *verstehen*. Because the questions are flexible the participant can expand on areas she feels are important, allowing the researcher to see things through her eyes. This in turn will improve validity, since the participants will open up and be truthful. In Source B the interviews lasted for around an hour, showing that the women had plenty of time to expand on their answers, and it shows that a friendly rapport was established, and that the women were given a voice. In a topic such as this it is important since within a 'lad culture' women may often feel muted.

84   OCR A-level Sociology

Example 2 questions

Another strength of semi-structured interviews to investigate 'lad culture' is that they are ethical. Instead of asking set questions or making assumptions, they allow each participant to tell her own story. Even though it is a sensitive topic, full consent is gained, unlike if observations of lad culture were carried out, and also it allows the participants to ask questions too. The researchers say that reflexivity was carried out, meaning that they involved the participants in the research, answered their questions and considered the impact of the research on them, seeing the participants as collaborators rather than subjects. More structured questioning techniques are sometimes seen as exploitative, since they just take information from the participants, whereas this was more a two-way process, which interpretivists would see as more ethical.

The main weakness of semi-structured interviews is that they are unreliable. This is because they do not have standardised procedures, since their questions can vary, so they cannot be repeated and checked. Positivists would not agree with this since they value reliability and a more scientific approach to research. No claims can be made about the findings since they cannot be replicated due to each interview being different.

A final weakness of semi-structured interviews is that because they are time-consuming and in-depth, they are usually done on a small scale. This means the sample is not likely to be representative, and the findings cannot be generalised to a wider target population. Positivists would therefore not value this method, since they aim to make generalisations. In Source B, only 21 interviews were carried out, alongside four focus groups, so this sample is much too small to be representative of the target population of women in HE. Though the researchers did try to make the sample diverse, including disabled women, and those from different ethnicities and sexualities, the majority were white, middle-class and heterosexual, therefore not reflecting the target population.

In conclusion, interpretivists would definitely see semi-structured interviews as useful to study this topic, since they would dismiss the weaknesses positivists raise. They do not aim to generalise, or make any scientific claims, so issues of validity and ethics are much more significant than reliability and representativeness. In a personal and sensitive topic such as lad culture and sexualisation of women on university campuses, such an interpretivist approach is the most appropriate and effective.

These points are all well explained and supported with concepts and theory, and linked effectively to the source.

This is a well-explained weakness, but does not link to the source or the context. Aim to link every point to the topic mentioned and/or illustrate it with reference to the source.

This is a better weakness in terms of context — well illustrated using Source B. It is also fully explained, using concepts and theory.

This conclusion does a good job in focusing back on the question, linking back to the context of the research and fully demonstrating the debate between interpretivists and positivists and their research aims.

The overall response is excellent, with three well-explained strengths and two well-explained weaknesses. This is enough to access top marks. Though one of the weaknesses is not linked to the source/context, there are some excellent links, including in the conclusion, so there is enough for full marks.

25/25 marks awarded

Questions & Answers

> **Student answer**
>
> 5   One way in which gender impacts on life chances relates to the workplace. Women's chances of getting good pay and promotion are affected by their gender in comparison to men, as shown by the gender pay gap and the glass ceiling and vertical segregation. Vertical segregation means that within certain industries, the top jobs are dominated by males and the bottom jobs by females. One example would be the airline industry where pilots tend to be male and cabin crew tend to be female. This is linked to the glass ceiling, where women can climb to a certain point up their career ladder, but then meet a barrier. All this contributes to the gender pay gap, which is around 18% and can be seen across many employment sectors.
>
> Another inequality in the workplace particularly affects the life chances of working-class males. There has been a feminisation of the labour market which means that traditional male industries such as manufacturing, shipbuilding, steelworks and mining have all declined, creating large-scale unemployment for working-class males and therefore limiting their life chances. At the same time the service sector has thrived, so that job opportunities for women have increased. This can lead to a crisis of masculinity according to Mac an Ghaill.
>
> A second area is crime. Males are disadvantaged due to stereotyping and so are much more likely to be stopped and searched and arrested. This links to the chivalry thesis. Pollak argues that women are treated more leniently by the police and courts and let off, and they also hide their crimes due to being devious. This shows that males' chances of being arrested and imprisoned are higher based on gender.
>
> A final area is education. Females are disadvantaged in terms of subject choice. Skelton found they are more likely to be encouraged towards arts and humanities subjects, and away from STEM subjects. This impacts on their later job opportunities and earning potential, linking to horizontal segregation, since fewer women work in engineering and technology, where jobs have higher pay and status, but more work in the caring professions which have lower pay and status. In education males may also be disadvantaged, however. They tend to get lower grades at GCSE and are less likely to go to university. This may relate to anti-school subcultures, such as the macho lads of Mac an Ghaill, and the view that working hard at school is not seen as masculine. This relates to Archer and Yamashita and the pressure on boys to demonstrate hyper-heterosexuality, which means not working hard at school, but mucking around instead, which will limit their later prospects.

In a question relating to 'life chances', make sure you focus on this wording and on the impact of the inequalities you outline on a group or individual's actual chances of achieving something. This paragraph does this will by linking to the 'chances' of getting good pay and promotion, and by making a comparison to males.

This is an excellent response. Three clear areas of social life — work, crime and education — are covered, and there is at least one developed piece of evidence for each one. Aim for at least four different pieces of evidence in total, and get the right balance between range and depth. Each of the points is supported with specific evidence in the form of studies and concepts, and clearly applied back to the impact on life chances, which is a key part of the question.

20/20 marks awarded

Example 2 questions

Student answer

6 Weberian explanations of inequality are based on the ideas of Max Weber. Though he did not specifically discuss age inequality, his explanations of inequality and those of other Weberians can be applied to inequalities faced by both older and young people.

Weber's three sources of inequality are class, status and party. By class, Weber meant a person's market position, and the marketable skills they have, which will determine their power to earn money. Older people could be seen as lacking class or earning potential in UK society because their skills are often seen as out of date, and they are also stereotyped by employers as having less energy and competence, according to Ray. Additionally, young people also suffer from lack of 'class' due to their lack of work experience and stereotypes about young people being lazy. Therefore Weber would argue that lack of marketable skills is a key reason for older and younger people suffering discrimination, in comparison to those in the middle age group, who dominate the higher-paid positions in society.

The second aspect of Weberian explanations for inequality is status. This refers to your prestige and how you are seen in society, and can also come from status symbols, based on consumption patterns. Older people have low status because no one wants to be old, so they are not a group people look up to in the UK. This is not true in all societies, and Turner points out that in small-scale societies where the main value is wisdom, older people often have high status. However, in Western societies where we value money and youth, older people have low status, which can explain their inequality of treatment compared to other age groups. Parkin would argue that they are a negatively privileged status group, and that the middle age group operates social closure in order to maintain their status at the expense of the older generation. This can also apply to the young, who are also socially excluded and denied full rights and status. In addition, the status of elderly and young people will vary as they intersect with other aspects of status according to Vincent, such as gender, social class and ethnicity. Older women often have lower status than older men, and also young and old people from the working class have lower status.

> Depth and detail are achieved in this paragraph by using several sociologists to link to Weber's idea of status.

Weber's final idea of party is less relevant today, but it can be argued that older and younger people have less access to powerful contacts and organisations which can give them power. This can link to neo-Marxist Bourdieu's concept of social capital. Young people are the least likely group to be in trade unions for example, and both old and young people are under-represented

Researching and understanding social inequalities 87

Questions & Answers

in politics and in business. Also, when older people retire they lose their links to their workplace, reducing their membership of influential groups. This lack of party means that issues affecting older and younger people are often not fully represented in society, since they have less influence.

However, other theories would challenge Weberian ideas and suggest different explanations for the inequalities faced by older and younger people. Functionalists would tend to use their concept of meritocracy to explain inequalities, and so instead of blaming other people's perceptions of older people and young people, like Weberians do, they would blame their own lack of skills or effort. This is supported by Cummings and Henry who argue that older people are no longer so beneficial to society, so it is functional for them to disengage. So it is not a lack of earning power or status but an actual lack of ability which justifies their inequality.

Feminists explain age inequality by looking at how older women are treated as losing their femininity, due to the menopause, and also losing their attractiveness. Itzin argues that because women's status in society is linked to their biology and to childbirth, when they are past childbearing age they are no longer valued. This can link back to Weberian ideas of status, and be used to support Weberian arguments about the lack of status explaining older people's inequalities.

Another Weberian idea that can be applied to explain age inequality is Baron and Norris's dual labour market theory. The primary labour market refers to full-time, permanent careers, which have promotion prospects. Young workers, especially students, are not usually in jobs like this, they are in the secondary labour market comprising low-status and low-paid jobs, often involving zero-hours contracts and few rights. Young people also have a lower minimum wage. The reason for this might be because employers assume that young workers are less committed, and also that they do not need the money because they are still living with their parents. Older workers may also be in the secondary labour market, since Phillipson found that jobs available to older people are less desirable. Both older and younger workers are more likely to be in 'lopaq' jobs, which stands for low-paid, part-time and with no qualifications, which are secondary labour market jobs. Reasons for this are because both age groups may be more prepared to take these jobs since they are less likely to have mortgages to pay and families to support, but also because of employers' assumptions about

---

In some areas of inequality there is a slight lack of range of specific theorists or ideas, and age tends to fall into this category. This student has done well to create range by separating out and applying class, status and party, and also adding depth by linking to other Weberian ideas and concepts.

This is an explicitly evaluative paragraph which avoids the common mistake of merely juxtaposing a different theory. Here the student shows exactly what it is about Weberian views which is challenged by functionalists and why.

This paragraph is in danger of being juxtaposition — merely stating another view on age inequality. However, at the end it is linked back to support Weberian ideas on status, so does gain credit for AO3. It could be more fully developed, however.

them, that they are less hard-working or committed. For example, research by CV-Library found that over half of under-18s felt they are not taken seriously at work.

However, these ideas may be outdated. Postmodernists such as Featherstone and Hepworth would argue that age is less important these days and the different stages in the life-course are not so clear cut. There are many examples of older people doing important jobs, such as Trump who is president in his 70s, and also young people setting up and running successful companies, such as Mark Zuckerberg. Therefore, Weberian views on lack of status are not true anymore and anyone can do what they want to do.

In conclusion, because Weberian explanations include a range of sources of inequality, they can be effectively applied to explain age inequality and work for both old and young people. The intersection with gender, class and ethnicity can also be incorporated into Weberian explanations, due to the concept of relative status. However, in today's fast-moving society age is more fluid, so postmodernists may be right when they argue that age is becoming much less important as a source of inequality.

This conclusion does more than simply summarise what has already been written — which is a common approach to writing conclusions. It actually makes a judgement, pulling out the best features of the Weberian view but also the most convincing challenge to its relevance.

Overall, this is a good essay, with all points being well supported with sociological concepts, theorists and studies. It has four clear and detailed ideas relating to Weberian views, which are well applied to age inequality throughout, so scores full marks for AO1 and AO2. The evaluation, though explicit, lacks in range and is slightly underdeveloped in places — you should aim for at least four detailed evaluative points supported with evidence — so the AO3 mark is slightly lower, though the conclusion helps, and takes it to near the top of level 3 for AO1, with 11 out of 16 marks available.
35/40 marks awarded

The student scores 95 marks out of 105 for this paper.

Questions & Answers

■ Example 3 questions

Section A

Read the source material and answer **all** the questions in Section A.

Source A

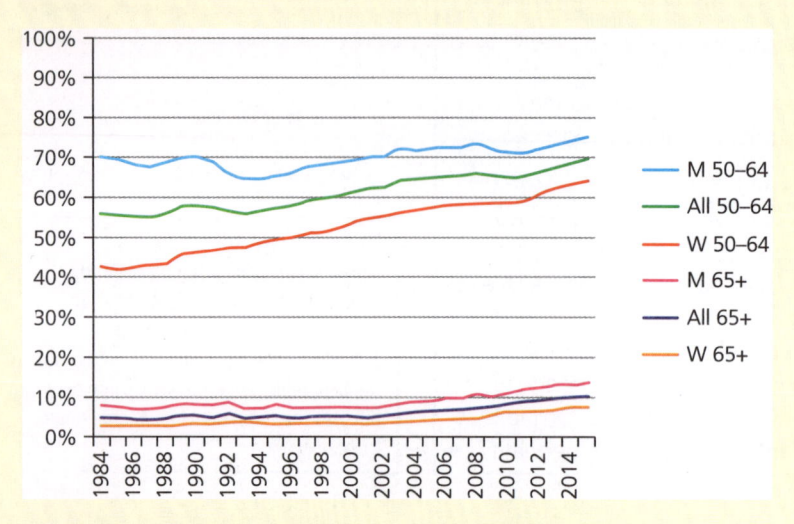

Employment rates for people aged 50–64 and 65+
Source: Department for Work and Pensions (November 2015)

Source B

Women's perceptions of equality in the twenty-first century

The Fawcett Society commissioned Ipsos MORI (a research organisation) to conduct qualitative research to understand what equality feels like and means to women in the twenty-first century. They conducted semi-structured interviews which were ethnographic in the sense that they included elements of participant observation. The research was published as a film on YouTube, as well as in a written report. The film shows excerpts from the interviews, which took place over a period of time mostly in the women's own homes, and also observes the women going about their day-to-day lives.

The researchers selected eight women participants based on 'portraits' they created, to ensure they included a range of ages, ethnicities, educational and occupational backgrounds and viewpoints. However, they make clear that their research is not intended to be 'representative'. In order to select women to fit their portraits, they asked two initial attitudinal questions to potential participants: to what extent they felt that equality with men had been achieved, and whether they thought they had a non-'traditional', contemporary lifestyle or whether they had assumed a more traditional gender-determined role, aiming to include women with a range of responses to these questions. They also attempted to achieve diversity based on a range of relevant characteristics such as employment status, income and socioeconomic group, care responsibilities, age, relationship/family status, ethnicity and sexuality. They recognise, however, that while they tried to include the greatest demographic diversity possible, they were constrained by the realities of a small sample size.

Through the ethnographic approach and the way the findings were presented the researchers aimed to let the women speak for themselves. They grouped the women's views broadly into the themes of 'education', 'work/life balance' and 'financial independence' since these were the themes which most came through from all the women as significant.

The researchers found that there were two key points of transition in women's lives which impact on perceptions (and the realities) of equality in the longer run.

First, the transition from secondary to tertiary education:

'…when I went to enrol, [they suggested] beauty therapy, art and design things like that, no, like, oh why don't you do this…like carpentry or something like that…try it see if you like it…I'd probably really enjoy it if I did…but I don't think there's education or publicity going out there to say to women, oh you can be up there or you can earn a lot more, why don't you just try this… (Skye)

'when you're at uni, it's like, obviously you get educated in a subject but you also get educated in life in general…you know, it's such a transformation…but it actually does change the way you think…you see your tutor and she's like a strong lady with like a strong personality and it changes your mind, your view and perspective as a woman in general, it's like, I want to be my tutor…that's when independence kicked in and it was like right, yeah, this is something good, I like this feeling… (Neelam)

Secondly, the decision to have a family:

'…it's not sharing. It's a nice idea…but actually the reality is that all the drain physically, mentally, emotionally — first and foremost — is 80% women, 20% guys…being at home is still quite a trade off, and it's a huge adjustment…' (Heidi)

'…if I had my time again I would have pursued what I wanted to do. But things got in the way …it was the children…and you can't seem to stay focused on what you want to do.' (Susan)

Source: Adapted from Suzanne Hall and Chris Perry (2012) '"…who has that": Women's perceptions of equality in the 21st century', The Fawcett Society and Ipsos MORI Social Research Initiative; used with permission

Questions & Answers

Question 1

Summarise two patterns or trends shown in Source A. 4 marks (AO2)

> Don't forget to illustrate each point with actual data.

Question 2

With reference to Source A, explain two reasons why quantitative data may be used by researchers studying employment rates in terms of age and gender. 6 marks (AO1: 2 marks; AO2: 4 marks)

> Make sure each reason is illustrated with reference to Source A.

Question 3

With reference to Source B, explain one strength and one weakness of the sample used to study women's perceptions of inequality. 10 marks (AO2: 4 marks; AO3: 6 marks)

> Make sure your two points are separated and both clearly link to Source B.

Question 4

Using Source B and your wider sociological knowledge, assess the usefulness of an ethnographic approach to researching women's perceptions of equality. 25 marks (AO1: 5 marks; AO2: 5 marks; AO3: 15 marks)

> Demonstrate your understanding of what 'an ethnographic approach' is and present strengths and weaknesses linked to Source B and the context of the question.

Section B

Answer **all** the questions in Section B.

Question 5

In what ways is age a source of inequality in the workplace? 20 marks (AO1: 12 marks; AO2: 8 marks)

> This question focuses just on workplace inequalities. This is the only area of social life that could be specified in a question, since it is explicitly referred to in the specification. You need to ensure you cover a range of points, at least four, and consider inequalities for older and younger people.

Question 6

Discuss the view that gender inequalities are fair and natural. 40 marks (AO1: 16 marks; AO2: 8 marks; AO3: 16 marks)

> You will need to work out which theory or theories would agree with the view in the question, and present and apply these to gain AO1 marks, using other theories to challenge this view in evaluation.

Example 3 questions

Student answer

1. One trend is that employment rates have increased for everyone over 50 since 1984.

   One pattern is that males work more than females in both age categories.

> This response correctly identifies one trend and one pattern, but gives no data to support either, so only gains half marks.
> **2/4 marks awarded**

Student answer

2. Quantitative data consist of numerical information and are usually collected on a large scale. Positivists would use such data because they produce patterns and trends, such as in Source A where patterns in terms of gender and age can be seen relating to employment. This makes it easy to represent in a graph, and see clearly patterns such as that males are employed more than older females. It is on a large scale, often based on the whole population, so it is representative and generalisable. Employment statistics are produced by the government, and official statistics are a good source of quantitative data which are easy and free to use. Because they are produced in a standardised way, they can be repeated regularly, allowing trends to be identified in employment, and this also means they are reliable.

> There are some good points here, but they are not clearly separated into two ways, but instead are presented as several related points. It is worth thinking carefully, before you start, how to structure your answer into two clear points, then develop each of these. This is linked to the source throughout, though is verging on lip service at times. It gets 1 out of 2 marks for AO1 and 3 out of 4 marks for AO2.
> **4/6 marks awarded**

Student answer

3. One strength of the sample used in Source B is that it aimed to be diverse to give a range of different viewpoints. The researchers ensured diversity in terms of age, family status, ethnicity and so on, which is important when looking at gender inequality, since a woman's social situation will impact on her views. They also aimed for some women who were more positive about equality and some who were more negative to reflect the whole range. Interpretivists might say this is a purposive sample, because it deliberately selected people with certain characteristics to gain a fuller insight into the topic.

   One weakness of the sample is its representativeness. The researchers admit that it is not representative and this is mainly because of the small sample size — only eight women. It is not possible to say that eight women are a cross section of all UK women, which means the findings are not generalisable to the target population. Positivists would argue this is not useful, since they aim to generalise and identify patterns and trends, which this sample does not allow you to do.

> This is an excellent answer which clearly identifies a strength and a weakness, directly linked to the source, and illustrates both with reference to theory and methodological concepts.
> **10/10 marks awarded**

Questions & Answers

Student answer

4   An ethnographic approach is taken by some interpretivists who want to understand a way of life, and usually involves spending a lot of time with the people being studied. In Source A the researchers used semi-structured interviews but also participant observation, because they filmed the women going about their daily lives. One strength of this is that it would give high validity. Because they were also being observed it would show the link between what they say and what they were actually living, ensuring validity, which is why an ethnographic approach is better than just interviews alone, according to interpretivists. The interviews were quoted and it let them speak for themselves, which shows validity.

> This is an excellent paragraph which shows understanding of the methodological approach in the question, and links directly to the source, developing the concept of validity well and using theory.

However, this approach is time consuming and not very practical. It is clear that the research took place over a long period of time, and would have been costly, since an ethnographic approach requires a high level of commitment from the researchers involved. For this reason it is usually done on a small scale — in Source B it only focused on eight women, and it would have been impossible to do this kind of research on a much bigger sample. Due to this, positivists would not find it useful since it lacks representativeness and cannot be generalised, so does not really give the views of all women.

Another strength is that an ethnographic approach allows the researchers and participants to build up a good rapport. As it took place over a period of time they would have got to know each other and felt comfortable opening up. This would also allow for *verstehen*, since the researchers can see through the women's eyes. Doing the observation and filming the women's daily lives also helps give *verstehen* since you can see what it is actually like for them. This would also improve the validity. Because the women were interviewed in their own homes where they felt comfortable, they would open up and the researchers would get a detailed and true picture of how the women really felt about equality.

However, another criticism of this approach would be that the information is not reliable. Each of the interviews was different, since they were semi-structured and therefore would have different questions depending on the responses. This means they cannot be repeated on another sample of women and gain similar results. The observations would also be unreliable. Positivists not would find this research useful because of this, since the data produced are not reliable, scientific or objective, since they may be a result of leading questions and the interviewer effect.

> It is important to stay focused on the question, and the 'ethnographic approach', rather than just evaluating specific methods. This student mostly achieves this. Some of the points are slightly lacking in development — for example, the part at the end about the interviewer effect could be expanded. However, there is enough range here with clear strengths and weaknesses and the engagement with the source is excellent. This gets 5 marks for AO1 and AO2 based on the accuracy of knowledge and application to the source, and 13 out of 15 marks for a good range of strengths and weaknesses, but slightly lacking in development of the two weaknesses.
> **23/25 marks awarded**

Example 3 questions

Student answer

5   One way that age creates inequality for younger workers relates to pay and conditions. Young people are the only workers where it is legal to pay them less for the same work. The minimum wage is lowest for those under 18, then different for those aged 18–21 and for those under 25. Younger people are also more likely to be on apprenticeships, where the pay is even lower. Barron and Norris would link this to the dual labour market, arguing that young workers are more likely than older workers to be in the secondary labour market, featuring low-paid and low-status jobs. This also links to the gig economy, where a lot of newly created jobs are temporary and based on zero-hours contracts, and these are more likely to be done by younger than older workers, meaning they have few rights and little protection at work.

Another source of inequality for young people is that they have much higher rates of unemployment than the rest of the working age population. In 2019 the youth unemployment rate was over three times higher than the overall unemployment rate. Marxists might link this to the use of young workers as a reserve army of labour, where they are used to fill in gaps in the labour force, especially at Christmas and in the summer when other workers want to spend time with their families, but then pushed out again.

> By making comparisons back to 'the rest of the working age population' the student ensures focus on the question — inequality must be shown in relation to another group.

When young workers are employed they may also experience discrimination. Loretto et al. found that they experience lower pay and negative attitudes relating to their skills and commitment than workers in their thirties and forties. This is supported by research from the CV-Library website which found that over half of workers under 18 say they are not taken seriously at work. These stereotypes may come from media portrayals of youths as lazy and irresponsible.

Older people may also experience inequality in the workplace. Ray found that employers often assume older workers are less competent than those of middle age or below, though studies show no actual evidence of lack of competence. A *Dispatches* documentary, 'Too Old to Work', highlighted this: employers often said that they wanted workers who were dynamic and flexible, which was discriminatory towards older applicants. CV-Library's research backs this up and found that one third of workers claimed that they had been rejected for a job because of their age. The digital divide may also affect job opportunities and career progression for older workers, since they may lack the online skills required to find jobs. Jenkins found that in the hotel industry, recruitment usually took place via internet, which could prevent older people from applying. Jenkins also found that the corporate image of the hotels may have meant that older workers, who were seen as less attractive, were not given jobs.

> This is quite a narrow question, but it is still important to get a range of points, even though there is only one area of social life involved. By considering both older and younger workers, and looking at issues including recruitment, pay and types of jobs, this answer manages to get a good range of points, supporting all with evidence, and therefore gains full marks.
>
> **20/20 marks awarded**

Researching and understanding social inequalities

Questions & Answers

Student answer

6 This view would be supported by functionalists. Parsons argues that men have a naturally instrumental role and are suited to being the breadwinner and protector. However, women have a naturally expressive role, more suited to nurturing children. These views suggest that women should be less focused on their career and more on their family based on their natural abilities, justifying inequalities in terms of pay and progression. It can also explain horizontal segregation, since women are best suited to the caring professions due to their expressive role. Sociobiologists such as Tiger and Fox would support Parsons, arguing that we have a human biogrammer, which in terms of evolution still programmes men to be the providers and women to be the carers. Durkheim agrees that this division of labour is functional for society.

Referring to sociobiologists is one way of adding depth to this functionalist explanation about gender roles being 'natural'.

These biology-based views are challenged by radical feminists who argue that biology is always used as the basis of women's oppression, but this is just a way to justify inequality. Shulasmith Firestone argues that men have developed a power psychology, since they enjoy their power over women, using biology as a basis to discriminate. This is not natural superiority, but just because in patriarchal society males are reluctant to give up this power so use biology to maintain it. She argues that the only way to create equality is to free women from the nuclear family and childbirth. Therefore Firestone would disagree that gender inequalities are fair and natural, but say they are created by men and patriarchy.

These two paragraphs use different strands of feminism to challenge the functionalist view, but both are well focused and avoid simply juxtaposing different views. Keep linking back to the wording in the question to achieve this focus, especially when evaluating.

Liberal feminists would also challenge the functionalist arguments that gender inequalities are fair and natural, arguing that they are learned through socialisation rather than natural. Oakley argues parents bring up their children in gendered ways, through manipulation and canalisation. This can include the way they play with their children, the activities they do, the clothes and toys they give them and so on. Therefore girls learn to be more submissive and less ambitious, often being criticised for being bossy, for example, and boys learn to be assertive. These traits may affect women in their education and their careers and also create stereotypes in the minds of employers. Therefore these inequalities later in life are not fair and natural, but are learned through socialisation.

Parsons also discusses human capital. This is the build-up of work-related skills and attitudes which are valued by employers. Men build up more human capital since they are unlikely to take time off during their career to have children, and are more career-focused and ambitious. Women are less committed to their careers and their main source of identity is their family role.

Therefore they are less committed to work. Thus Parsons would argue that it is fair that female employees are paid less and given fewer promotions than male employees. This is based on meritocracy, not gender discrimination.

Marxist feminists would disagree with Parsons' ideas about this being fair. Benston argues that women are more likely to be part of a 'reserve army of labour' hired by the capitalist class when the economy is prospering but laid off when not needed, and this is not fair or natural, but a way of exploiting both male and female workers more and preventing them from building up human capital. Marxist feminists Dalla Costa and James argued that caring and housework should be recognised and paid. Women work just as hard but their domestic work is not fully valued by capitalist society, which is not fair.

Two more good paragraphs, which use concepts as well as names to debate the view.

Another theory which supports the view is the New Right. Phyllis Schlafly argues that marriage and motherhood are women's main priorities, based on their biology, and that women's main purpose is to be a good wife and mother. She sees this as a positive and fulfilling role and disagrees with feminists that women should have equal opportunities in the workplace. Males are the ones who should have all the career opportunities since their role is to financially support their family. Therefore, she also agrees that gender inequalities, such as horizontal and vertical segregation and the domestic division of labour, are both fair and natural. Women should see marriage and motherhood as their most important roles and accomplishments.

A supporting view comes from Catherine Hakim with her rational choice theory. She argues that women choose to have children and know that this means prioritising them above their careers and suggests that most women are happy with this. Men and women have different work orientations — most adult women still accept the sexual division of labour. This means women have weaker commitment to work than men and often choose to give up, go part-time or take on a lower status, lower stress job when they have a family. She argues that 20% of women are home-centred, 60% are adaptive, managing family around part-time work, and only 20% are work-centred. However, if they could afford it, Hakim thinks many mothers would work even less than they do. Based on this, Hakim would agree with Parsons that it is fair that employers recognise this difference in priorities and treat women employees less favourably.

By splitting these two paragraphs, this student helps to show that they are slightly different points, though linked, and therefore increases the range of points they will be credited for.

Feminists challenge the ideas of Schlafly and Hakim. Ginn argues that Hakim is oversimplifying things, since for many women prioritising family is not a choice but a necessity, since they are required to cut back on their work due to unequal

Questions & Answers

parental leave arrangements. Hakim is not recognising that men do not have to make this choice and can have a family and a career. Therefore, Ginn would not agree that inequalities are fair and natural but are the result of patriarchal society which shapes the attitudes and choices of women and men and promotes stereotypical expectations.

In conclusion, the argument that gender inequalities are fair and natural seems outdated and unjustifiable. There is a lot of evidence that women can compete with men in all walks of life, and now we have shared parental leave men are starting to recognise the importance of the parenting role as well. Both functionalists and feminists may be challenged for not allowing women the choice, but in today's postmodern society both men and women should benefit from more enlightened views and recognise that natural differences do not necessarily split along gender lines.

This is an excellent essay. The evidence in support of the view is well focused throughout and supported with relevant theorists. Evaluation is explicit, focused and supported with evidence and there is a clear conclusion. This essay gets full marks.
40/40 marks awarded

The student scores 99 marks out of 105 for this paper.

Knowledge check answers

1. Patterns are links between variables shown in the data, for example patterns in terms of gender, social class or age. Trends are changes over time shown in the data, for example an increase or a decrease.
2. Positivists take a scientific approach to research so it is important to them that research is standardised and replicable, and can show that however many times it is carried out, the findings will be the same and so can be depended upon.
3. Researcher imposition refers to the problem of the researcher 'imposing' their values or assumptions on the research design. Positivists would seek to avoid this, to ensure that research is not biased in any way. This relates to value freedom — research which is free from any values the researcher, or those funding the research, may have.
4. In the text the example used is the link between gender and youth crime. Select any other aspect of sociology and create a research aim, a hypothesis and some research questions.
5. Interpretivists favour qualitative research, in which respondents are encouraged to elaborate on their answers and questions are not structured or standardised. This allows the meaning of different concepts to be explored throughout the research, and therefore the precise operationalising of concepts in individual questions is less important.
6. A pilot study would be important for a structured questionnaire or interview to ensure that the standardised questions are clear and accurate. It would be less important for a semi-structured or unstructured interview, where questions can be modified to address any issues raised during the interview.
7. Interpretivists are more likely to adopt respondent validation. This is because the qualitative data collected will often be summarised or organised into themes, and so it is useful to ask the respondent whether this still gives a true representation of what they said or what happened.
8. A suitable sampling frame could be a membership list from a local gym or fitness centre.
9. The main advantage is its representativeness — it is the most likely sampling technique to produce a fully representative sample. The disadvantages are mostly practical: it is difficult and time-consuming to create a stratified sample.
10. A quota sample is the most likely to achieve a representative sample since it attempts to ensure that appropriate proportions of people with different characteristics, which reflect the target population, are chosen.
11. Such an interview gives the respondent a voice, and allows them to explore their experiences and feelings, without imposing any judgements through predesigned questions. Interpretivists, especially feminist researchers, would see this as ethical. This assumes the respondent has given fully informed consent and the privacy and confidentiality of the respondent have been protected.

    However, some may argue that researching such a sensitive topic may expose the respondent to psychological harm and distress, making it unethical.
12. The class pay gap is the gap in pay experienced by those in the same job and with the same qualifications and experience, based on their social class background.
13. Examples could include feedback on tests and homework, effort grades and setting students based on their 'ability'. Each of these may be used to reinforce that outcomes are based on ability and effort, and that everyone has an equal chance to do well.
14. Both functionalists and the New Right suggest that an individual's social class position is based on their own levels of hard work and effort, and their norms and values.

    Both theories also suggest that it is functional for some to do less well than others — for example, to get lower grades in education or to get paid less at work — because society needs different levels of people doing different jobs.
15. Ideas about status and consumption can be linked to postmodernists, who argue that consumption has replaced production as our main source of social class identity and status.
16. Subject choice in education, the gender balance of role models within different occupations and continuing media stereotypes all contribute to the maintenance of horizontal segregation. Research the recent example of Esme Summers, who thought only boys could be firefighters until her mum asked for female firefighters to get in touch on social media.
17. Feminists may argue that we are all brought up to accept patriarchal ideology — the male-dominated view of the world — and so women such as Hakim and Shlafly have accepted these views of women's roles, not realising that they are imposed on them by patriarchy.
18. A woman may relieve a man's stress and frustration by looking after the domestic side of things, so he feels calm in the home, and by listening to his complaints about work, making him feel that he has a voice. In some cases she may soak up his frustration more directly, through becoming a target of emotional, psychological or physical abuse.
19. Some feminists see laddism and sexism as a 'backlash' since, as females have challenged male dominance and power in education and the workplace, males may seek other ways to challenge and undermine women, and maintain their superior position and status in society.

Knowledge check answers

20 Evidence of the ethnic penalty and Jenkins' study on recruitment practices, for example, both illustrate the lack of promotion prospects and concentration in lower paid and lower status jobs experienced by workers from certain minority ethnic groups, which will lead to vertical segregation. Ashong-Lamptey's research supports this, suggesting that there will be a limit to how high those from some ethnic backgrounds can climb in their careers.

21 Assimilation requires the understanding and adoption of the host culture's norms and values. However, it is arguably impossible to adopt a culture, for example, learn a language and a lifestyle, if the hosts will not mix with you and help you to feel you can fit in.

22 Marxists might see racism as benefiting capitalism because it divides working-class people and makes them easier to control, it creates 'scapegoats' for white working-class people to demonise and blame for social problems, and it ensures a powerless group which can be used as a reserve army of labour.

23 This term refers to the recognition of the intersections between gender, social class, ethnicity, age and so on, suggesting that women or men cannot be thought of as one homogeneous group. This is related to issues of ethnic inequality by black feminists, since women of colour face disadvantages when compared to white women in the UK, meaning that more traditional feminist views cannot be applied to all women.

24 Parsons and Cummings and Henry are suggesting that older people have less to contribute to society in terms of their skills and roles, which could be supported by the idea that due to the generational digital divide, in a fast-moving, digital age, older people and their experience are less relevant.

25 Both young and old have been used as a reserve army of labour. Young people, and students in particular, often fill in gaps in the labour force by taking on work during peak times. Older people often seek temporary work after retirement to top up their income. This kind of work is often paid at lower rates and attracts fewer rights and benefits than in the full-time labour market.

26 Younger people may lack the skills and experience to attain jobs in the primary labour market, and both age groups may be more likely and willing to take on jobs in the secondary labour market, since they have fewer financial commitments and may appreciate the flexibility of temporary or zero-hours contracts, for example, as such jobs may fit round studying commitments for younger people and be a step towards retirement for older people. Employers may also make assumptions about the commitment and reliability of older and younger workers, and thus be less prepared to offer them jobs in the primary labour market.

27 On television, older women are less visible as presenters or newsreaders, even though older men are often seen in these roles — you could do some content analysis of TV shows, noting down the age and sex of different presenters. Also, consider whether there are as many high-profile film roles for older women as there are for younger women or older men.

Index

Note: page numbers in **bold** indicate key term definitions.

A

access
   to groups for research 10, 17
   to official statistics 23
age inequalities 59–68
   feminist explanations 66–67
   functionalist and New Right explanations 61–63
   in health 60–61
   Marxist explanations 63–64
   Weberian explanations 64–66
   in the workplace 59–60
alienation **64**
Ansley, women's role in supporting capitalism 39, 46
Ashong-Lamptey, lack of minority ethnic groups in professions 50
assimilation **52**
attractiveness, young women 66, 67

B

Banyard, Kat, *The Equality Illusion* 49
Barron and Norris, dual labour market theory 37–38, 44, 48, 56
Beauty Myth, The (Wolf) 67
Beechey, Marxist feminist 38
Bell Curve, The (Murray and Herrnstein) 52
Benston, Marxist feminist 46
bias
   interview bias 22
   participant observation 28
   researcher imposition 8–9
   selection bias 15
black feminism 57–58
Bowles and Gintis, 'myth of meritocracy' 36

C

capitalism 35–36, 38, 53–54, 63–64
Castles and Kosack, exploitation of immigrants 53, 54, 55
class, Weberian source of power 36–37
   and age inequality 64, 65
   and ethnic inequality 55, 56
   and gender inequalities 43
Collins, Patricia Hill, black feminist 57–58
confidentiality 18
content analysis 23–24
covert participant observation 27–28
Cox, 'racism' is socially constructed 53
cultural capital **36**
cultural explanations for ethnic inequality 51
   evaluation of 52–53

D

Dalla Costa and James, domestic labour 46
data collection 6, 12
data interpretation 12–13
Davis and Moore, education and role allocation 32
de Beauvoir, Simone, on ageing 66
dependency culture, Murray 34, 52, 62
'disengagement theory', Cummings and Henry 62
dual labour market theory 44
dual labour market theory, Weber **37–38**
   criticism of, Bradley 45
   liberal feminist ideas 48
   relation to age 65
'dual systems' of patriarchy and capitalism, Walby 38, 67
Durkheim, Émile 32, 36, 42, 51

E

education
   and meritocracy 52
   and social class inequality 32, 33, 36
empathy 8
Equal Pay Act (1970) 40

Equality Act (2010) 64
ethics in research 17–19
   exploitation of research participants 19
   illegality and immorality 18–19
   informed consent 18
   privacy and confidentiality 18
   protection from harm 18
ethnic inequalities 49–58
   cultural explanations 51, 52–53
   feminist explanations 56–58
   functionalist explanations 51–52
   Marxist explanations 53–55
   New Right explanations 52–53
   structural explanations 51
   Weberian explanations 55–56
   in the workplace 49–51
ethnic penalty **50**
ethnography 24–25

F

false consciousness **35**, 36
feminine mystique 45–46
Feminine Mystique (Friedan) 45
feminisation of labour **41**
feminist explanations
   age-related inequalities 66–67
   ethnic inequalities 56–58
   gender inequality 45–49
   social class inequality 38–39
Firestone, Shulasmith, 'sexual class system' 47
Friedan, Betty 45–46
functionalist explanations
   age inequality 61–63
   ethnic inequality 51–52
   gender inequality 42, 43
funding of research 10

G

Gannon, ageing process 66–67
gatekeeper **17**, 27
gender inequalities 40–49
   feminist explanations 45–49
   functionalist explanations 42
   Marxist explanations 43–44

Researching and understanding social inequalities 101

Index

New Right explanations 42–43
Weberian explanations 44–45
in the workplace 40–41
gender pay gap **40**
generalisability 9, 14–15
'gig economy' **38**
glass ceiling **40**

H
Hakim, Catherine, women's rational choices 48
health inequalities
for older people 60–61
and social class 32
Heath and Cheung, 'ethnic penalty' in labour markets 50
Hockey and James, 'infantilisation' of older people 65–66
hooks, bell, black feminist 55
horizontal segregation **40**, 44, 46, 48, 49
human capital **42**, 43
hypothesis 11

I
ideological state apparatus (ISA), Althusser 36
illegality, research ethics 18–19
illegitimacy, Murray 34, 52
immigrant communities/workers
evaluation of cultural explanations 52–53
functionalist views 51–52
Marxist perspective of workers 53–54
immorality, research ethics 18–19
income inequality *see* pay gap
informed consent, research ethics 18
institutional ageism **60–61**
interpretivism 7–9
criticism of questionnaire use 21
critique of structured interviews 22
data interpretation 12–13
ethnographic method 24–25
meanings and experiences 8
participant observation 28
qualitative data 8
reflexivity 9
researcher imposition 8–9
sceptical of official and non-official statistics 23
subjectivity 9
validity 8
verstehen, empathy and rapport 8
intersectionality 44, 48, 57, **67**
interview bias **22**
interviews
semi-structured 26
structured 21–22
unstructured 25–26

J
Jenkins, recruitment practices 50, 59

L
liberal feminism 45–46, 48
longitudinal studies 13

M
Marçal, Katrine, *Who Cooked Adam Smith's Dinner?* 46
Marxist explanations
for age-related inequality 63–64, 66
for ethnic inequality 53–55
for gender inequality 43–44
social class inequality 35–36
Marxist feminism 46–47, 48
means of production **35**
meritocracy **32**, 36, 42, 52
methodological pluralism 29
micro approach, Weberians 65–66
Miles, racism and racial inequality 54
Millet, Kate, patriarchal ideology 47
mixed methods 29
Murray, Charles
dependency culture 34, 52, 62
ethnicity-intelligence link 52
lone-parent families 34, 42
and the 'underclass' 33–34, 35

N
negatively privileged status groups **55**, 64
New Right explanations
for age inequality 61–63
for ethnic inequalities 52–53
for gender inequality 42–43
social class inequality 33–35
non-official statistics 22
strengths and weaknesses of 23
non-participant observation 26–27

O
Oakley, liberal feminist 43, 45
comparing women and children 67
objectivity **7**, 9
observations 26–28
official statistics 22
strengths and weaknesses of 23
old boy network **44**
older people
'disengagement theory' 62
health inequalities 60–61
workplace inequalities 59–60
Olsen and Walby, women's lack of human capital 43
operationalisation **11**
opportunity sampling 16
overt participant observation 27

P
Parkin, negatively privileged status groups 55, 64
Parsons, Talcott
on age inequality 61–62
ideas on meritocracy 32, 52
sexual division of labour 42
participant observation 27–28
party, Weberian source of power 37
and age inequality 65
and ethnic inequalities 55–56
and gender inequalities 44–45

Index

patriarchal ideology 45, 46, **47**, 48
patriarchal values 7
Patterson, host immigrant model 51–52
   evaluation of 52–53
pay gap
   age-related 60, 63, 65
   class-related 31–32
   gender-related 40–41, 44, 48, 49
'personhood', loss of 65–66
Phillipson, older people 59–60, 64
pilot studies 12
positivism 6–7
   objectivity and value freedom 7
   patterns and trends 6–7
   quantitative data 6
   reliability 7
postcolonial theory 57
primary data 12
privacy issues, research ethics 18
protection from harm, research ethics 18
purposive sampling 16

Q
qualitative data 8
   content analysis generating 24
   ethnographic research 24
   interpretation of 12–13
   mixed methods 29
quantitative data 6
   content analysis 23–24
   mixed methods 29
   non-participant observation 26
   questionnaires 19–21
   structured interviews 21
questionnaires 19–21
quota sampling 16–17

R
racialised class fractions 54
racism 51, 53, 54, 55, 57, 58
radical feminism 47, 48
random sampling 15

rapport 8, 22, 25, 26, 28
reflexivity, interpretivists 9, 13
reliability 7
representativeness 9, 14
   and sampling techniques 15, 16
repressive state apparatus (RSA), Althusser 35
research methods 19–30
   content analysis 23–24
   ethnography 24–25
   mixed methods 29
   observations 26–28
   questionnaires 19–21
   semi-structured interviews 26
   statistical data 22–23
   structured interviews 21–22
   unstructured interviews 25–26
research process, key concepts 10–14
   aims of a study 10
   data collection 12
   factors influencing choice of topic 10
   hypotheses 11
   interpretation of data 12–13
   longitudinal studies 13
   operationalisation 11
   pilot studies 12
   primary and secondary data 12
   research questions 11
   respondent validation 13
   sociology and social policy 14
research questions 11
research topic, factors influencing 10
researcher imposition **8–9**, 13
reserve army of labour **38**, 39, 46, 53–54, 60, 66
respondent validation 13
response rates **20**
Rex and Tomlinson, minority ethnic groups 56
Rowbotham, Sheila, capitalism and patriarchy 46–47

S
sampling frame 15
sampling process 14–15
   generalisability 14–15
   representativeness 14
   sampling frame 15
   target population 14
sampling techniques 15–17
   non-random 16–17
   random 15
Saunders, Peter 34, 62
Schlafly, marriage and motherhood 43
secondary data 12
selection bias **15**
semi-structured interviews 26
semiology **24**
Sexual Politics (Millett) 47
Shared Parental Leave Regulations (2014) 41
Sharpe, Sue, liberal feminist 46
snowball sampling 16
social capital **56**
social class inequality 31–39
   feminist explanations 38–39
   functionalist explanations 32–33
   in health 32
   Marxist explanations 35–36
   New Right explanations 33–35
   Weberian explanations 36–38
   in the workplace 31–32
social closure **37**
social desirability effect **22**
social policy 14
social reproduction of labour power **38**
statistical data 22–23
status, Weberian source of power 37
   and age inequality 64–66
   and ethnic inequality 55, 56
   and gender inequality 44, 45
   and social class inequality 37–38

Index

stratified (random) sampling 15
structural explanations for ethnic inequality 51
structured interviews 21–22
subjectivity **9**
superstructure **35**
surplus value **35**
systematic sampling 15

T
target population **14**
  sampling frame 15
theoretical approaches
  interpretivism 7–9
  positivism 6–7
triangulation 29
Turner, older people's status 65

U
underclass **33**, 35, 52, 56
undercover/covert observation 27–28
unstructured interviews 25–26

V
validity 8
value consensus **33**, 51
value freedom 7
verstehen **8**, 21, 22, 25, 26, 28
vertical segregation **40**, 41, 42, 46, 48, 49
Vincent, age stratification 65
volunteer sampling 16

W
Walby, Sylvia
  criticism of liberal feminism 48
  'dual systems' of patriarchy and capitalism 38, 67
  intersectionality 67
Weberian explanations
  for age inequalities 64–66
  for ethnic inequalities 55–56
  for gender inequality 44–45
  for social class inequality 36–38
Wolf, Naomi, women and attractiveness 67
workplace inequalities
  and ethnicity 49–51
  for females 40–41
  for males 41
  for older people 59–60
  relating to social class 31–32
  for younger people 60

Y
young people
  attractiveness-oppression link, young women/girls 67
  lower class, status and party 65
  rebelliousness of 63
  workplace inequalities 60
Young, scapegoating of the underclass 35

Z
zero-hours contracts 38, 44
Zuckerberg, Mark 64